# The Planet Organic Market
# Cookbook

# The Planet Organic Market
# *Cookbook*

*Good food.*
*Good for you.*
*Good for the Earth.*

## By Diane Shaskin

Planet Organic Market

Cover and Interior Design by Suburbia Advertising
Printed and bound in Canada.

Canadian Cataloguing in Publication Data

Shaskin, Diane
The Planet Organic Market cookbook: Good food,
Good for you, Good for the Earth / by Diane Shaskin.

Includes index.
ISBN 978-0-9783156-0-3

1. Cookery (Natural foods) I. Planet Organic Market II. Title.
TX741.S44 2007          641.5'63          C2007-905271-1

The Planet Organic Market Cookbook is printed
on FSC certified paper. The text pages contain
10% post-consumer recycled content.

**Mixed Sources**
Product group from well-managed
forests, controlled sources and
recycled wood or fiber
www.fsc.org  Cert no. SW-COC-1563
© 1996 Forest Stewardship Council
FSC
10%

# Dedication

*For friends, family and customers who have helped*

*to make a lifetime of food memories and to Mark Craft*

*who has shared my love of good food. And of course, for our*

*son Alexandre who makes every meal fun and memorable.*

# Contents

# Acknowledgements

*It certainly takes a village to create a cookbook, and in our case, the village is a big one! Thanks to the many women who helped shape this cookbook – Jeneen Harrison for sharing her recipes, Tine Prins for her efforts in preparing every single recipe during the hot months of summer, Heather Prins for tasting every single recipe and for her technical expertise. Of course, many thanks to our Planet Organic Team and Cooking Class Instructors who contributed their favourite recipes. To Nancy Bierlmeier and Jacquie Henning who kept the project going with their edits. I'd also like to thank one man – Bruce Meikle who helped my words flow as smooth as honey.*

# The Beginning

*Food, travel and people.*

*One day, as I stood in*

*a lineup at a mega-sized*

*grocery store, I thought to*

*myself there has to be a better*

*way! Grinding away at the*

*office only to stand in a cold,*

*heartless grocery store was*

*no kind of life for me.*

In 1992, I set upon finding my future. I nailed down my three passions – food, travel and people. I told all my friends that I was interested in opening a café and kitchen shop. A few weeks later, Sally told me that she heard the health food co-op was for sale.

The deal took minutes to put together. I gave notice at CBC-TV, where I was working as a production coordinator. Friends and family thought we were nuts. At the time, layoffs were an everyday occurrence at the CBC. Quitting felt like liberation.

The co-op was dirty, rundown and poorly stocked. It did, however, have a kitchen and 6 café chairs, brick walls and high ceilings. The building, a heritage site dating from 1897, had originally been a grocery/hardware store. I was elated – I knew this was it!

The first days at the store were surreal. I had no retail experience, had never operated a cash register and didn't know the first thing about "health foods."

In the stockroom, we discovered we had purchased twenty 10-gallon containers of maple syrup, 3 tonnes of hard red winter wheat and 300 bottles of apple cider. We created a special recipe for cookies that used maple syrup as a major ingredient. We also stacked the bags of wheat on a trolley, and each day we had a "special" on wheat – it took about 2 years to sell it all.

I walked around the store with a clipboard and wrote down customer requests – things like Kamut and brown rice syrup, things I had never heard of. We started to stock the shelves and clean, clean, clean. Within weeks, people began to notice. I loved the exhilaration of our sales climbing and the daily positive response. It was like winning an Oscar every week!

Within a few months, we had started the renovation on the store. I wanted the store to feel like an Italian grocer you might chance upon in Tuscany – high shelves, low tech, colourful, warm lighting. In fact, to this day, our stores integrate most of the elements from our earliest designs.

The renovation was a labour of love. We put a second mortgage on the house to finance it. I learned I was good at this – I liked talking to customers and finding out what foods they love and how whole foods had created a new level of health and vitality in their lives.

Customers became my greatest teachers – I learned how their children's allergies had forced them to become savvier food shoppers, I met with customers whose cancer, arthritis and other ailments had moved them into the organic food movement.

And I learned to appreciate the service that our store offered to them. Our store had become part of their community. Friends met and lingered over the bulk bins, or joined each other to attend our cooking classes. Our store had become an important meeting place in our neighborhood.

From the beginning, the love of good, healthy food has brought people together at Planet Organic. As such, we have always shared favourite recipes in our stores, in our newsletter and on our website. And since the only thing more inspiring than a great recipe is to taste something you can't wait to make, our popular in-store delis have generated countless requests for recipes from our customers.

This book is my way of continuing this important tradition of sharing. These recipes have been gathered from staff, friends and customers – and they include many favourites from our delis. Even as we have grown from one store to locations across Canada and into the U.S., our goal and our motto haven't changed: "Good food, good for you, good for the earth."

I hope, in its small way, this collection of well-loved recipes will help you find the same in your life.

–**Diane Shaskin,**
*Co-founder and Marketing Director*
*for Planet Organic Markets*

PLANET ORGANIC
CERTIFIED ORGANIC
Collard Greens

PLANET ORGANIC
CERTIFIED ORGANIC
Red Chard

PLANET ORGANIC
CERTIFIED ORGANIC
Green Cabbage

PLANET ORGANIC
CERTIFIED ORGANIC
Bunch

# 1

# The 10 Best
# Things to Eat
## *on Our Planet*

Of all the dozens of things we serve in our Planet Organic delis, these are the best of the best. Many of these recipes have long been sought by our regular customers, and we're very happy to finally share them with you. For those of you who have never tasted them, you'll soon find out why they are so popular. And if you've enjoyed these dishes in our store, you'll be pleasantly surprised by how easy they are to make at home.

PLANET
ORGANIC
M A R K E T

# Beet and Fennel Salad

*Fennel is the much more interesting Italian cousin of celery. With a mild anise/licorice taste, the crunchy fennel bulb adds a crispy, unique taste to this salad.*

## Ingredients:

| | | |
|---|---|---|
| 3 lbs | Beets, whole | 1.5 kg |
| 1/4 cup | Green onions, thinly sliced | 60 ml |
| 1/2 cup | Fresh parsley, chopped | 125 ml |
| 2 tsp | Dill, dried | 10 ml |
| 1 - 2 cups | Fennel, thinly sliced | 250 - 500 ml |
| | Shallot Dressing (see page 62) | |

## Method:

Trim ends off beets and place in a large pot. Cover with water and bring to a boil. Reduce heat and simmer 20-30 minutes or until tender.

Remove from heat and rinse under cold running water to remove skins. Slice or chop beets and combine with remaining ingredients. Dress with Shallot Dressing (see page 62). **Yields 8 servings.**

### Beets

Beets owe their bright plummy colour to the antioxidant betacyanin – an anti-aging molecule that slows the oxidization of cells. But despite their wrinkle-fighting capabilities, beets are high in essential nutrients including calcium, potassium and folic acid (making them great for pregnant women). Some holistic practitioners believe that beet juice combined with carrot and cucumber are excellent for cleansing the kidneys and gallbladder and for restoring health.

# Blackened Tofu Steaks

*Who would guess that tofu tastes better Cajun style? Chef Paul Prudhomme's Blackened Steak Magic is the secret ingredient we use to turn tofu into meaty, tasty steaks. This is tofu even a meat lover will enjoy.*

### Ingredients:

| | | |
|---|---|---|
| 1 lb | Tofu, firm | 500 g |
| 1/4 cup | Blackened Steak Magic | 60 ml |
| 1/4 cup | Extra virgin olive oil | 60 ml |

### Method:

Preheat oven to 400°F. Slice tofu into thin steaks. Mix oil with Blackened Steak Magic to create a paste. Spread over tofu covering all sides.

Place on a baking tray and bake 15-20 minutes turning once.
**Yields 2-4 Servings.**

# Spinach Mushroom Lasagne

## Ingredients:

| | | |
|---|---|---|
| 9 | Lasagne noodles, dried | 9 |
| 2 tbsp | Extra virgin olive oil | 30 ml |
| 2 lbs | Mushrooms, sliced | 1 kg |
| 2 tbsp | Garlic, minced | 30 ml |
| 2 cups | Ricotta cheese | 500 ml |
| 1 lb | Frozen spinach, thawed, drained well | 500 g |
| 1 tsp | Sea salt | 5 ml |
| 1/4 tsp | Freshly ground pepper | 1 ml |
| 2 cups | Mozzarella cheese, grated | 500 ml |
| 1/2 cup | Parmesan cheese, grated | 125 ml |
| 2 cups | Marinara sauce (see page 5) | 500 ml |

*Our popular meat-free lasagne is everything you want lasagne to be: hearty, delicious and filling.*

### Spinach

No wonder Popeye loved spinach so much! This super vegetable is loaded with flavonoids and carotenoids to help prevent aging, function as antioxidants and fight some cancers, including prostate and breast cancer.

## Method:

Preheat oven to 350°F. Bring a large pot of salted water to a boil and add pasta noodles. Cook 5-8 minutes. Remove from heat and drain. Toss with a dash of oil so they don't stick. Set aside.

In a medium-sized saucepan, heat oil, add mushrooms and garlic and cook over medium heat 10 minutes. Remove from heat and cool.

When cooled, add spinach, ricotta cheese, salt and pepper. Mix until well combined. Mix the mozzarella and Parmesan cheeses together and reserve 1/4 cup. Spread 1/4 cup of marinara sauce on the bottom of the lightly oiled 9"x13" baking dish.

Layer 3 noodles. Top with 1/2 of the spinach/ricotta mixture. Press down firmly before proceeding. Spread half of the mozzarella/Parmesan mixture and then 3/4 cup of marinara sauce.

Repeat for one more layer. Place remaining noodles on top, then spread 1/4 cup marinara sauce and top with the reserved cheese mixture. Cover with foil and cook at 350°F for 40 minutes. Uncover and cook until cheese is browned. Let rest for 15 minutes before serving. **Yields one 9"x 13" pan.**

# Marinara Sauce

## Ingredients:

| | | |
|---|---|---|
| 3 tbsp | Canola oil | 45 ml |
| 2/3 cup | Onions, diced | 160 ml |
| 2 tbsp | Garlic, minced | 30 ml |
| 1 tsp | Freshly ground black pepper | 5 ml |
| 1 tsp | Sea salt | 5 ml |
| 2 tsp | Basil, dried | 10 ml |
| 2 tsp | Oregano, dried | 10 ml |
| 2 tsp | Thyme, dried | 10 ml |
| 28 oz can | Tomatoes, crushed | 796 ml |

## Method:

In a large saucepan, sauté onions and garlic in oil until soft.

Add remaining ingredients and bring to a boil.

Reduce heat and simmer until sauce reduces and gets thick (approximately 1 hour), stirring occasionally. **Yields 2 cups.**

# Spinach Poppy-seed Salad

*This recipe proves that pasta salad isn't just for your next retro 80's party. The veggies keep the pasta from weighing you down, and the coleslaw dressing is light and flavourful.*

## Ingredients:

| | | |
|---|---|---|
| 1 lb | Favorite short pasta, cooked and cooled | 500 g |
| 4 cups (1 bunch) | Baby spinach, fresh, washed | 1 L (1 bunch) |
| 1 | Red onion, thinly sliced | 1 |
| 1 | Red pepper, thinly sliced | 1 |
| 1 tbsp | Poppy-seeds | 15 ml |
| | Coleslaw Dressing (see page 58) | |

## Method:

Cook pasta in a large pot of boiling, salted water 5-8 minutes or until al dente.

Combine cooled pasta with remaining ingredients and toss with dressing. Serve warm or chilled. Good for 2-3 days. **Yields 8 - 10 servings.**

# Spinach Potato Cakes

*We don't sell hotcakes, but our savoury spinach potato cakes sell even better. Why? Because these comforting cakes go well with everything from eggs for breakfast, a salad for lunch or turkey basil loaf for dinner.*

## Ingredients:

| | | |
|---|---|---|
| 2 lbs | Yukon gold potatoes, diced | 1 kg |
| 1/2 cup | Extra virgin olive oil | 125 ml |
| 1/4 cup | Onion, diced | 60 ml |
| 2 tsp | Garlic, minced | 10 ml |
| 1 tsp | Rosemary, fresh or dried | 5 ml |
| 10 1/2 oz | Frozen spinach, thawed & chopped | 300 g |
| 1 cup | Feta, crumbled | 250 ml |
| 1/2 cup | Parmesan, grated | 125 ml |
| 2 | Eggs | 2 |
| 1 tsp | Oregano, dried | 5 ml |
| 1/2 tsp | Sea salt | 2 ml |
| 1 tsp | Freshly ground black pepper | 5 ml |
| 1 1/2 cups | Bread crumbs | 375 ml |

## Method:

Steam or boil potatoes until soft. Mash and set aside to cool.

In a large skillet over medium heat, cook onions and garlic in oil until soft (about 10 minutes). Set aside to cool.

In a large bowl, combine cooled potatoes, onion mix and all remaining ingredients until well mixed. Scoop or form mixture into 3/4-inch patties.

Pan-fry patties in a small amount of oil on medium heat for a minute on each side to create a crust. Place on a baking sheet and bake in a preheated 350°F oven for 15-20 minutes. Remove from oven and enjoy hot. **Yields 12 cakes.**

# Steamed Greens with Arame Seaweed

## Ingredients:

| | | |
|---|---|---|
| 1/2 cup | Arame seaweed | 125 ml |
| 1 bunch | Chard, chopped and rinsed | 1 bunch |
| 1 bunch | Kale, chopped and rinsed | 1 bunch |
| 2 cups | Broccoli florets | 500 ml |
| 1/4 cup | Bragg Liquid Aminos | 60 ml |
| 2 tbsp | Toasted sesame oil | 30 ml |
| dash | Chili flakes | dash |
| 1 tbsp | Gomashio | 15 ml |

## Method:

Place arame in a medium bowl and pour boiling water over top. Set aside to reconstitute for 5 minutes.

Steam chard, kale and broccoli 5-8 minutes. Drain arame and toss with steamed greens and all remaining ingredients. Enjoy hot or cold. **Yields 4 servings.**

## Gomashio Ingredients:

| | | |
|---|---|---|
| 1 cup | Sesame seeds | 250 ml |
| 1 - 2 tsp | Sea salt | 5 - 10 ml |
| 1 tsp | Sea kelp powder | 5 ml |

## Method:

In a dry, heavy frying pan, heat sesame seeds, salt and kelp on medium–high for 3-5 minutes, stirring constantly until seeds are lightly browned. Remove from heat and let cool.

Place in a coffee grinder, blender or food processor and grind for 3 seconds. Don't grind into a powder, just enough to crush the seeds. Store in a shaker.

*Many people balk at kale, and seaweed and broccoli aren't always everyone's favourite, either. But put them all together with a tangy dressing, and something magic happens. We cannot keep up with the demand for this unbelievably healthy salad!*

### Kale
Kale is a wonderful health-promoting leafy green vegetable loaded with flavonoids and sulfur-containing phytochemicals.

### Gomashio
Gomashio is a traditional Japanese seasoning made from toasted unhulled sesame seeds and salt that is easy to make and handy to have.

# Tofu Sesame Snacks

**Bragg Liquid Aminos**

Non-fermented Bragg Liquid Aminos taste just like soy sauce, but with much less sodium than its traditional counterpart. Plus, this gluten-free liquid protein concentrate is certified GMO-free and safe for Candida diets!

*Who ever thought mild-mannered tofu could have such...attitude? Many have tried to crack the code on our savoury peppery snack, and now they'll become a favourite in your kitchen.*

## Ingredients:

| | | |
|---|---|---|
| 1 pkg | Tofu, extra-firm pressed | 400 g |
| 3 tbsp | Bragg Liquid Aminos | 45 ml |
| 3 tbsp | Toasted sesame oil | 45 ml |
| 3 tbsp | Sesame seeds | 45 ml |
| 1 tsp | Cumin, ground | 5 ml |
| 1/2 tsp | Freshly ground black pepper | 2 ml |

## Method:

Preheat oven to 350°F. Slice tofu into sticks and toss with remaining ingredients. Allow to marinate 30 minutes or overnight.

Place tofu on a baking tray and bake 15-20 minutes or until golden brown. Remove from oven and enjoy hot or cool. **Yields 24 sticks.**

# Turkey Basil Meatloaf

*This is thoroughly modern meatloaf. Made with turkey, it has much less fat than most meatloaves. It also features basil to add a fresh flavour to an old friend.*

## Ingredients:

| | | |
|---|---|---|
| 3 lbs | Ground turkey, organic | 1.5 kg |
| 1 cup | Onions, diced | 250 ml |
| 1 cup | Bread crumbs | 250 ml |
| 1 tbsp | Oregano, dried (not ground) | 15 ml |
| 2 tsp | Parsley, dried | 10 ml |
| 1 tbsp | Garlic, minced | 15 ml |
| 1/2 tsp | Freshly ground black pepper | 2 ml |
| 1 1/4 tsp | Sea salt | 6 ml |
| 1 | Egg | 1 |
| 1/2 cup | Fresh basil, chopped | 125 ml |
| 1/4 cup | Tomato sauce or ketchup | 60 ml |

## Method:

Preheat oven to 350°F. Prepare 9" x 5" loaf pan.

In a large bowl, combine all ingredients except tomato sauce or ketchup. Place into the loaf pan and cover with foil and bake for 45-60 minutes or until no longer pink inside (internal temperature of 180°F).

Remove foil and spread top of loaf with sauce or ketchup and bake an additional 10 minutes.

Remove from oven and allow to rest for 10 minutes before cutting.
**Yields 6 - 8 servings.**

# Wild Rice and Pecan Salad

*This wonderful salad combines the nutty flavour of wild rice with chunks of toasted pecan, brightened by the crunch of red and yellow peppers. Our famous ginger soy dressing adds a very nice sweet/salty finish.*

## Ingredients:

| | | |
|---|---|---|
| 1 cup | Wild rice, dry | 250 ml |
| 1 cup | Brown rice, dry | 250 ml |
| 1/4 cup | Fresh parsley, chopped | 60 ml |
| 1/4 cup | Green onions, thinly sliced | 60 ml |
| 1/2 cup | Pecan pieces, toasted | 125 ml |
| 1/4 cup | Currants | 60 ml |
| 1 cup | Red pepper, thinly sliced | 250 ml |
| 1 cup | Yellow pepper, thinly sliced | 250 ml |
| | Ginger Soy Dressing (see page 60) | |

## Method:

Cook both types of rice in separate pots as per package instructions or until done. Drain and cool.

Combine cooled wild rice and brown rice with remaining ingredients. Dress with Ginger Soy Dressing (see page 60). Best served chilled. **Yields 4 servings.**

# Wild Teriyaki Salmon

*Wild salmon doesn't need a lot of help to create a great dish. Using our popular Ginger Soy Dressing as a marinade adds a blend of Asian flavours that complements the salmon perfectly.*

## Ingredients:

| | | |
|---|---|---|
| 2 lbs | Wild salmon | 1 kg |
| 1 cup | Ginger Soy Dressing (see page 60) | 250 ml |

## Method:

Preheat oven to 350°F. Prepare baking sheet with parchment paper or aluminum foil.

Slice salmon into 5-ounce portions or leave side whole. Place in a non-reactive dish, pour dressing over salmon and let sit 5-15 minutes.

After marinating, place salmon on a lined baking sheet and bake for 15-25 minutes or until fish flakes with a fork. Serve immediately or chilled. **Yields 6 servings.**

### Seafood

Fish and other seafood are nutritious partners in any meal; salmon is low in saturated fat, high in protein and loaded with heart-smart omega-3 fatty acids. Studies have shown that omega-3 fatty acids promote general heart health and can contribute to lowering blood pressure.

Salmon is also an excellent source of vitamins A, D, B6 and B2 and contains all of the essential amino acids.

Belgian Chocolate
Brownies

Cosmic Cookies

Carrot Spelt Cake
with Cream Cheese Icing

Chocolatey Vegan
Cupcakes with Vegan
Chocolate Glaze

Banana Bread

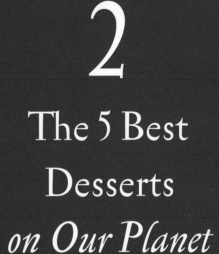

# 2
# The 5 Best
# Desserts
## *on Our Planet*

Some people say "life is short – eat dessert first!" We're not sure that's true, but we do know that many people first try out the Planet Organic deli because of our incredible range of treats.

There's nothing as irresistible as goodies that are also good for you, and these 5 recipes are the best loved and most irresistible of all.

So if your cooking time is short, why not make some dessert first?

PLANET
ORGANIC
M A R K E T

# Belgian Chocolate Brownies

*From a country best known for beer and bureaucrats, rich Belgian organic chocolate can do so much for a brownie. And the nice part of brownie baking is that the hardest part is melting the chocolate. This recipe is one of our bakers' favourites.*

## Ingredients:

| | | |
|---|---|---|
| 2/3 cup | Butter | 160 ml |
| 1/4 cup | Brewed coffee | 60 ml |
| 1 3/4 cups | Dark chocolate chips | 430 ml |
| 3 | Eggs | 3 |
| 1 cup | Granulated cane sugar | 250 ml |
| 1/4 cup | Unbleached white flour | 60 ml |
| 1 cup | Walnuts or pecan pieces (optional) | 250 ml |

## Method:

Preheat oven to 350°F. Line a 9"x 9" pan with parchment paper.
Put butter and coffee in a heavy-bottomed saucepan over low heat until butter is melted. Turn off heat and add chocolate. Let stand 3 minutes and then stir until smooth. Set aside.

Beat eggs and sugar. Add chocolate mixture, flour and walnuts (optional) and continue to mix until combined, scraping sides to incorporate all flour. Pour into prepared pan.

Spread evenly and bake for 35 minutes. Refrigerate overnight before cutting. **Yields 9 servings.**

# Cosmic Cookies

**Sunflower Seeds**

Sunflower seeds are power-packed with healthy fats, protein, fibre, minerals and vitamin E for a healthy circulatory system and to increase cellular repair.

**Oats**

Oats have loads of fibre and nutrients.

*We debated long and hard on whether or not to reveal this secret recipe. By far our most popular cookie, in one week the Edmonton deli sells more than 1500!*

## Ingredients:

| | | |
|---|---|---|
| 2 1/4 cups | Quick cooking oats | 560 ml |
| 2 cups | Spelt flour | 500 ml |
| 1 cup | Sunflower seeds | 250 ml |
| 3/4 cup + 2 tbsp | Pumpkin seeds | 210 ml |
| 1/2 cup | Shredded coconut, unsweetened | 125 ml |
| 1/4 cup | Flax seeds | 60 ml |
| 1 cup | Granulated cane sugar | 250 ml |
| 1 tbsp | Cinnamon, ground | 15 ml |
| 2 1/4 tsp | Sea salt | 11 ml |
| 1 3/4 cups | Dark chocolate chips | 430 ml |
| 1 1/4 cups | Raisins | 310 ml |
| 1/4 cup | Water | 60 ml |
| 1/4 cup | Blackstrap molasses | 60 ml |
| 3/4 cup | Canola oil | 180 ml |
| 1 cup | Soy milk | 250 ml |

## Method:

Preheat oven to 350°F. Line baking trays with parchment paper.

In a large bowl, combine dry ingredients, everything from oats to raisins. In a separate large bowl, combine wet ingredients, everything from water to soy milk. Add wet ingredients to dry ingredients and mix slow at a low speed (or by hand) until just combined. Do not over mix.

Portion cookie dough using a 1/3-cup measure and place onto lined baking tray. Gently flatten cookies before baking. Bake for 24 minutes or until lightly browned. **Yields 24 cookies.**

# Carrot Spelt Cake

*There may be no more comforting food than carrot cake with cream cheese icing. After all, is there a nicer way to eat your veggies and your dessert at the same time? This cake has another healthy difference: it uses spelt flour.*

## Ingredients:

| | | |
|---|---|---|
| 3/4 cup | Canola oil | 180 ml |
| 1 cup | Brown sugar | 250 ml |
| 3 | Eggs | 3 |
| 2 1/2 cups | Carrots, grated | 625 ml |
| 1 cup | Pineapple, crushed | 250 ml |
| 1/2 cup | Walnuts, chopped | 125 ml |
| 2 1/4 cups | Spelt flour | 560 ml |
| 2 1/4 tsp | Baking soda | 11 ml |
| 2 1/4 tsp | Baking powder | 11 ml |
| 1 tsp | Cinnamon, ground | 5 ml |
| 1 tsp | Sea salt | 5 ml |
| 1/4 cup | Walnuts, chopped and toasted (optional) | 60 ml |
| | Cream Cheese Icing (see page 19) | |

## Method:

Preheat oven to 325°F. Prepare one 13"x 9" or two 9" round cake pans.

In a mixer or large bowl, combine oil, sugar and eggs. Add carrots, pineapple and walnuts and mix on low speed until well mixed.

Add flour, baking soda, powder, cinnamon and salt and mix on low speed or by hand until well combined. Pour batter into a greased pan and bake 20-35 minutes or until a toothpick inserted comes out clean.

Either leave plain or, for an extra special touch, frost with Cream Cheese Icing (see page 19) and garnish with toasted, chopped walnuts. Cool completely before icing. **Yields one 13"x 9" cake or two 9" round cakes.**

# Cream Cheese Icing

**Cooking Tip:**

If you are making a layer cake, simply multiply the ingredients by 1.5.

### Ingredients:

| | | |
|---|---|---|
| 1/2 cup | Butter, softened | 125 ml |
| 2 cups | Cream cheese, softened | 500 ml |
| 1/4 cup | Pure honey | 60 ml |
| 1/2 tsp | Pure vanilla extract | 2 ml |
| 1 tbsp | Lemon juice | 15 ml |

### Method:

In a mixer, cream butter and cream cheese until smooth and free of lumps.

Add honey, vanilla and lemon juice and cream until well combined and fluffy. Spread on cake. **Yields enough icing for one 9" x 13" cake.**

# Chocolatey Vegan Cupcakes

*Imagine the perfect chocolatey cupcake. A cupcake so good that it deserves to be a secret cupcake recipe. This is that cupcake. Adored by vegans and omnivores alike, it's always been one of our best-sellers.*

## Ingredients:

| | | |
|---|---|---|
| 3 cups | Unbleached white flour | 750 ml |
| 2 cups | Granulated cane sugar | 500 ml |
| 1 cup | Fair trade cocoa powder | 250 ml |
| 2 tsp | Baking soda | 10 ml |
| 1 tsp | Sea salt | 5 ml |
| 1/2 cup | Canola oil | 125 ml |
| 2 cups | Cold water | 500 ml |
| 2 tbsp | White vinegar | 30 ml |
| 2 tsp | Pure vanilla extract | 10 ml |
| | Vegan Chocolate Glaze (see page 21) | |

## Method:

Preheat oven to 325°F. Prepare cupcake tins by greasing or with paper liners.

In a large bowl, combine all dry ingredients and stir until there are no lumps. Add the liquid ingredients and stir by hand until batter is smooth.

Divide batter evenly into the prepared pan. Bake for 20-30 minutes until top springs back when touched or until a toothpick, when inserted, comes out clean. Cool completely. Ice with Vegan Chocolate Glaze (see page 21). **Yields 18 regular cupcakes.**

## Variations:

### Vanilla Cupcakes
Omit cocoa powder and increase flour by 1 cup. Scrape seeds of one vanilla bean pod into dry ingredients and mix by hand to break the seeds up. Proceed with recipe.

### Apple Cinnamon
Omit cocoa powder and increase flour by 1 cup. Decrease water to 1/2 cup and add 1 1/2 cups applesauce. Add 1 tsp cinnamon. Proceed with recipe.

## Cooking Tip:
When making regular muffin-size cupcakes, an ice cream scoop works best to achieve even scooping.

# Vegan Chocolate Glaze

*This dairy-free, vegan topping is an easy and delicious substitute for traditional icing. It goes perfectly with our chocolatey vegan cupcakes (see recipe on previous page).*

## Ingredients:

| | | |
|---|---|---|
| 1/2 cup | Soy milk | 125 ml |
| 2 tsp | Vegan margarine | 10 ml |
| 1 cup | Dark chocolate chips, dairy-free | 250 ml |

## Method:

Heat soy milk and margarine. Pour over chips. Stir until melted and smooth.

Dip cupcakes and cool to harden glaze. Cover and keep in refrigerator. **Yields enough icing for 18+ regular cupcakes.**

# Banana Bread

*Many people don't like their bananas anything but bright yellow, but a delicious organic banana should never go to waste – even if has lots of freckles. This banana loaf is guaranteed never to be a doorstop – it's tender, light and delicious.*

## Ingredients:

| | | |
|---|---|---|
| 1 1/2 cups | Bananas, mashed | 375 ml |
| 2 cups | Demerara sugar | 500 ml |
| 2 tsp | Lemon juice | 10 ml |
| 1 tsp | Sea salt | 5 ml |
| 2 | Eggs | 2 |
| 2/3 cup | Canola oil | 160 ml |
| 3/4 cup | 2% milk | 180 ml |
| 2 1/2 cups | Unbleached white flour | 625 ml |
| 1 1/3 tsp | Baking soda | 8 ml |

## Method:

Preheat oven to 375°F degrees. Prepare two 9" x 5" loaf pans.

In a mixer or bowl, combine bananas and sugar. Mix well.

Add salt and lemon juice and mix.

Add eggs, mixing on low speed.

Add oil, milk, flour and soda; mix on low speed until combined.

Pour into two greased loaf pans and bake at 375°F degrees for 1 hour or until done. For last 15 minutes cover with foil to prevent bread from getting too dark. **Yields 2 loaves.**

# 3

# Feed Your
# Organic Sprouts –
## *Kids' Planet*

The earlier kids learn that good food doesn't come from a drive-thru lane, the sooner they'll learn healthy food habits. The recipes in this chapter are all heavily kid tested and totally kid approved. Even better, most of them are easy for kids to help out with or make on their own. The best way to get kids to eat healthy for the rest of their lives is to teach them to cook healthy when they're young.

PLANET
ORGANIC
M A R K E T

# Alexandre's Favourite Ginger Cookies

*Children love these cookies. They're light, simple and easy to make. Favourite shapes – gingerbread boys and girls.*

### Ingredients:

| | | |
|---|---|---|
| 1/2 cup | Butter, softened | 125 ml |
| 1/2 cup | Brown sugar | 125 ml |
| 1 | Egg | 1 |
| 1 tbsp | Water | 15 ml |
| 1 1/2 cups | Unbleached white flour | 375 ml |
| 1/4 tsp | Baking soda | 1 ml |
| 1/4 tsp | Sea salt | 1 ml |
| 1 tsp | Cinnamon, ground | 5 ml |
| 1 tsp | Ginger, ground | 5 ml |

### Cooking Tip

Oven temperatures can vary depending on make and model – always check cookies after 7 minutes; a "cool" oven can take up to 12 minutes. An added tip: unless you're one of the lucky few with perfectly balanced heat in your oven, remember to turn the pans front to back halfway through baking to ensure the cookies bake evenly.

### Method:

Preheat the oven to 350°F. Line cookie trays with parchment paper.

In a food processor or mixer, cream the butter and sugar together, then add the egg and water, and beat until light and fluffy.

Stir together the dry ingredients: flour, baking soda, salt, cinnamon and ginger. Add the first mixture and beat until the dough is completely mixed. Shape the dough into 2 equal-sized rolls, flour your hands and the work surface to keep the dough from sticking, wrap in wax paper and chill until firm for at least 30 minutes.

Turn out dough onto a lightly floured surface and roll to a thickness of about 1/3 inch. Cut out shapes and place about 1 inch apart on the cooking sheet. Reroll the remaining dough and cut shapes until all the dough is used. Bake for about 8-10 minutes until the cookies are lightly browned. Transfer to racks to cool. **Yields 4 dozen.**

# Crispy Cashew Butter Bars

*Rather than buying expensive pre-packaged health bars, why not make them? Even better, teach your kids to make them! They're very easy and kids love them. You can also use other nuts and nut butters — try almonds or peanuts.*

## Ingredients:

| | | |
|---|---|---|
| 2 1/2 cups | Crisped rice cereal | 625 ml |
| 1 1/4 cups | Rolled oats, slow cook | 310 ml |
| 1 cup | Mixed dried fruit, (unsulphured) chopped | 250 ml |
| 1 cup | Cashews, chopped | 250 ml |
| 3/4 cup | Brown sugar | 180 ml |
| 3/4 cup | Cashew butter, smooth | 180 ml |
| 3/4 cup | Pure honey | 180 ml |
| 1/2 cup | Fair trade cocoa powder | 125 ml |

## Method:

Prepare a 9"x 13" pan by lightly greasing bottom and sides.

In a large bowl, combine first four ingredients (rice cereal, rolled oats, chopped fruit and cashews) and set aside.

In a medium-sized heavy-bottomed saucepan, mix sugar, cashew butter, honey and cocoa and cook over low heat for 3 minutes.

Pour over dry ingredients and stir to evenly coat. Press firmly into prepared pan. Refrigerate until set (about 1 hour) before cutting into bars. **Yields 12 servings.**

# Earth Day Breakfast Pizza Crust

*More like a nutritious biscuit than a true pizza dough, this is a very easy recipe the kids will love getting their hands on.*

### Ingredients:

| | | |
|---|---|---|
| 1 cup | Unbleached white flour | 250 ml |
| 1/2 cup | Whole wheat pastry flour | 125 ml |
| 1 tbsp | Baking powder | 15 ml |
| 3/4 tsp | Sea salt | 3 ml |
| 1/4 cup | Butter, cold | 60 ml |
| 2/3 cup | Milk | 160 ml |

### Method:

Preheat oven to 450°F. Combine dry ingredients in big mixing bowl. Cut in butter with pastry cutter or two knives until mixture is of corn meal consistency.

Add milk and stir briefly until dough comes away from sides of bowl and holds together.

Turn out dough onto lightly floured board. Knead 10-15 strokes. Place dough on an ungreased baking sheet. Using floured hands, gently pat dough into a large, even circle 2/3" thick.

Bake 12-15 minutes until pastry is cooked in centre and golden brown. Remove from oven and allow it to cool slightly. **Yields 4 servings.**

# Earth Day Breakfast Pizza Topping

*If your kids are really hungry, why not feed them a whole planet? This educational and fun breakfast pizza can be decorated like our Earth. Just spread out the blueberries to represent water and use the kiwis to represent land. It's a great way to teach them about Earth Day, and it's a lesson that will stay with them long past lunchtime!*

## Ingredients:

| | | |
|---|---|---|
| 6 oz | Cream cheese | 180 ml |
| 1/4 cup | Apricot or strawberry jam | 60 ml |
| 5 | Kiwi fruit, thinly sliced | 5 |
| 2 cups | Blueberries, fresh, dried or frozen thawed | 500 ml |
| 2 tbsp | Pure honey | 30 ml |
| 1 tbsp | Lemon juice | 15 ml |

## Method:

Once the pizza base has cooled, spread with softened cream cheese. Using a spatula, spread a layer of jam over the cream cheese.

Place kiwi fruit slices, overlapping slightly, onto pastry to resemble land. Place the blueberries everywhere else – they're the ocean!

Dissolve honey with lemon juice and drizzle the honey-lemon glaze over the fruit. Slice into wedges to serve. **Yields 4 servings.**

# Eggless Egg Salad

*If your kids can't eat eggs because of an allergy, or just don't like them, this is a healthy and great-tasting sandwich filling.*

## Ingredients:

| | | |
|---|---|---|
| 1 pkg | Tofu, extra-firm pressed | 400 g |
| 1/3 cup | Red onions, chopped | 80 ml |
| 1/3 cup | Celery, chopped | 80 ml |
| 3/4 - 1 cup | Mayonnaise (vegan type) | 180 - 250 ml |
| 1 tbsp | Dijon mustard | 15 ml |
| 1/4 tsp | Sea salt | 1 ml |
| 1/4 tsp | Freshly ground black pepper | 1 ml |
| 1 tsp | Turmeric | 5 ml |

### Cooking Notes

If your child dislikes onions, replace them with extra celery. Just make sure to chop the celery to a fine texture.

## Method:

In a medium bowl, mash tofu until crumbly. Add remaining ingredients and stir together until combined.

Spread on your favorite sandwich bread or refrigerate until needed. **Yields 4 - 6 servings.**

# Energy Orbs

## Cooking Tip

For those with sensitive systems and an aversion to sulfites, it's worth buying unsulphured dried fruits – many health food providers include these in their bulk food sections.

## Variation

### Cocoa Orbs

Add 1/2 cup + 2 tbsp of organic cocoa into apple/apricot mixture.

*These are kid-friendly to make and very kid-friendly to eat. They've been a very popular source of energy in our deli for years.*

## Ingredients:

| | | |
|---|---|---|
| 1/2 cup | Apricots, dried and unsulphured (not bright yellow), minced | 125 ml |
| 1 cup | Apples, peeled, minced | 250 ml |
| 3 | Rice cakes, plain, crushed | 3 |
| 3 tbsp | Soy protein powder, plain | 45 ml |
| 1/3 cup | Quick oats | 80 ml |
| 1 cup | Coconut flakes, unsweetened | 250 ml |
| 1 1/2 tbsp | Sunflower seeds | 22 ml |
| 3 1/2 tbsp | Sesame seeds | 52 ml |
| 1/3 cup | Almond butter | 80 ml |
| 1/2 cup | Pure maple syrup | 125 ml |
| | Extra coconut for rolling | |

## Method:

In a food processor, chop apricots until minced. Set aside in a large bowl.

Process apples and mix with minced apricots. Add the remaining ingredients with the apple/apricot mixture until well combined.

Roll into 1/2" balls and toss in extra coconut to coat. Refrigerate for a couple of hours before serving. **Yields 4 dozen.**

# Pinky Potatoes

*Are your kids eating enough...pink? Seriously, changing the colour of familiar foods is a sure way to have more fun at every meal. These naturally dyed potatoes may turn pink or purple depending on the colour of your potatoes.*

## Ingredients:

| 20 | New potatoes, small | 20 |
|----|---------------------|----|
| 1/2 cup | Beet juice, or puréed beets | 125 ml |
| 1 tbsp | Extra virgin olive oil | 15 ml |
| handful | Fresh parsley, chopped | handful |
| to taste | Sea salt | to taste |
| to taste | Freshly ground black pepper | to taste |

## Variations

**Green Martian Potatoes**
Replace beet juice with puréed parsley.

**Angry Potatoes**
Replace beet juice with red peppers.

**Gold Digger Potatoes**
Replace beet juice with turmeric.

## Method:

Boil or steam potatoes until fork-tender (just cooked through).

Add in beet juice, olive oil and fresh parsley. Toss. Add salt and pepper to taste. **Yields 4 servings.**

# Roasted Potato Fries

## Potatoes

Potatoes have a bad reputation – but they're nutritional nuggets! Loaded with minerals, such as potassium and vitamin C, potatoes are a great way to get your daily dose of healthy fibre and iron.

## Cooking Tip

The variety of potato will vary cooking time – make sure that the potatoes are golden brown before turning over.

*Although kids find fries irresistible, deep-frying is time-consuming, potentially dangerous and not the healthiest thing you can do to a potato. But baking fries is easy, quick and only uses a small amount of healthy olive oil. The trick to making evenly browned fries is to line up the sliced potatoes on the baking pan in uniform lines. It makes them easier to flip – but don't turn them over until they're well browned.*

### Ingredients:

| | | |
|---|---|---|
| 6 medium | Russet potatoes, unpeeled | 6 medium |
| 1/4 cup | Extra virgin olive oil | 60 ml |
| to taste | Sea salt | to taste |
| to taste | Freshly ground black pepper | to taste |

### Method:

Preheat broiler to 400°F. Scrub and cut unpeeled potatoes into French fry wedges, generally 6-8 wedges per potato. In a large mixing bowl, mix oil and salt and pepper. Toss potato wedges to coat.

Line up potato wedges on large cookie tray. Bake for 10-15 minutes, until golden. Remove, turn over each potato slice. Put back in to the oven for another 5-7 minutes, until golden. Remove from oven, sprinkle immediately with sea salt and pepper. **Yields 6 servings.**

# Tropical Fruit Salad

*If you want a tropical experience without leaving home, this simple salad is a great dessert or a treat on a hot summer day. Get the kids to make it – it's something the whole family will enjoy. The combination of pineapple, papaya and cantaloupe is luscious!*

## Ingredients:

| | | |
|---|---|---|
| 2 cups* | Pineapple, peeled, cored and cut into 1/2-inch chunks | 500 ml |
| 1 cup | Papaya, peeled, seeded and cut into 1/2-inch chunks | 250 ml |
| 2 cups | Cantaloupe, cubed in 1/2-inch chunks | 500 ml |
| 1 cup | Seedless red grapes, halved | 250 ml |
| 1 cup | Seedless green grapes, halved | 250 ml |
| 1/4 cup | Coconut flakes, unsweetened (optional) | 60 ml |
| 2 tbsp | Pure honey (if fruit is not at optimal ripeness) | 30 ml |
| | Fresh mint sprigs | |

## Method:

Chop fruit into 1/2" uniform chunks and mix together in a large bowl. If fruit is not at its sweetest, add a dollop of honey. Cover; chill if serving later.

Use your imagination; feel free to substitute fruit if you can't find those listed here, but try to keep it tropical – kiwi fruit, star fruit and bananas would also work well. Best served at room temperature. **Yields 8 servings.**

\* Half of a pineapple is 2 cups

---

**Enzymes**

Fresh fruit contains natural enzymes that help to digest a heavy meal.

**Vitamin C**

Feeling low? Try some vitamin C! Cantaloupe, papaya and pineapple are great sources of vitamin C, which supports the body's immune system and helps protect the body against infection.

# 4

# And in the Beginning,
## *There Were Appies*

Whether you serve these to grateful guests or just treat yourself, these appetizers can be the beginning of a great meal. A few of them can also be combined very nicely to make a meal on their own. Even better, most of these recipes are very leftover-friendly, so one batch can be used to start multiple meals!

PLANET
ORGANIC
M A R K E T

# A Trio of Hummus

*We like hummus any way we can get it. So try the classic recipe as is, liven it up with the richness of roasted red peppers or try a green version by adding fresh, healthy spinach.*

## Ingredients:

| | | |
|---|---|---|
| 1 cup dry or 19 oz can | Chickpeas, dry or canned and rinsed | 250 ml dry or 540 ml can |
| 1 tbsp | Tahini | 15 ml |
| 2 tsp | Toasted sesame oil | 10 ml |
| 2 - 3 tbsp | Garlic, minced | 30 - 40 ml |
| 2 tbsp | Lemon juice | 30 ml |
| 1/3 - 1/2 cup | Extra virgin olive oil | 80 - 125 ml |
| 1 tsp | Sea salt | 5 ml |
| 1/2 tsp | Freshly ground black pepper | 2 ml |

## Method:

Cook chickpeas until soft. In food processor, mix all ingredients except olive oil until well blended. Add 1/3 cup olive oil and mix until all is incorporated.

Add remaining olive oil until desired consistency is reached. Adjust seasonings. **Yields 2 cups.**

## Hummus

This nutritious dip is packed with protein, dietary fibre and monoun-saturated fat – an incred-ible dip for vegetarians. Hummus is traditionally served with flatbread but can also be eaten with freshly cut vegetables.

## Variations

**Roasted Red Pepper Hummus**

Add 1-2 roasted red peppers to 2 cups of hummus and blend in food processor.

**Spinach Hummus**

Add 1 cup of fresh spinach to 2 cups of hummus and blend.

# Angeline's Med Bread

*This tomato-less bruschetta includes some of the heroes of the Mediterranean diet — olives, olive oil and garlic. Be sure to share it.*

Ingredients:

| | | |
|---|---|---|
| 1/4 cup | Extra virgin olive oil | 60 ml |
| 1 tbsp | Red wine vinegar or lemon juice | 15 ml |
| to taste | Sea salt | to taste |
| to taste | Freshly ground black pepper | to taste |
| 2 cloves | Garlic, minced | 2 cloves |
| 1/4 cup | Red onion, finely diced | 60 ml |
| 1/2 cup | Olives (your choice, a variety is nice), pitted and coarsely chopped | 125 ml |
| 1/4 cup | Roasted red peppers, coarsely chopped | 60 ml |
| 2 tbsp | Capers, chopped | 30 ml |
| handful | Fresh basil or parsley, coarsely chopped | handful |
| 1 | Narrow Italian bread or French baguette | 1 |

Method:

In a medium-sized bowl, mix olive oil, vinegar or lemon juice and salt and pepper and whisk well. Add garlic, onion, olives, peppers, capers and basil or parsley and mix well. Cover and let sit for at least 1/2 hour, and up to a day or two to allow the flavours to meld.

Cut the bread lengthwise and place under the broiler for approximately 1 minute, crisping the top, then spoon the mixture over it.

Another option is to cut the bread into little rounds and quickly pop the rounds under the broiler just until golden, then spoon each with some of the mixture. Alternatively, cut the loaf in half, cover with aluminum foil and heat thoroughly, cut and serve with the mixture (for a softer version of bread). **Yields 4 servings.**

# Coconut Yam Fritters

*These Asian-inspired fritters, developed for a Planet Organic Cooking class, are an excellent way to enjoy the sweet earthy taste and nutritional goodness of yams.*

## Ingredients:

| | | |
|---|---|---|
| 1/2 lb | Yams (about 1/2 of a large yam) | 250 g |
| 1/2 cup | Unbleached white flour | 125 ml |
| 1/2 cup | Rice flour | 125 ml |
| 1/2 tsp | Turmeric, ground | 2 ml |
| 1/2 tsp | Sea salt | 2 ml |
| 1/2 tsp | Baking powder | 2 ml |
| 1 cup | Coconut milk | 250 ml |
| | Canola oil (enough to pan-fry) | |

## Yams

We don't want to seem pushy, but everyone should eat more yams. Compared to other vegetables in terms of fibre content, complex carbohydrates, protein, vitamins A and C, iron and calcium, they're number 1.

In the yam vs. sweet potato naming contro-versy, this recipe refers to the moist-fleshed orange version of the sweet potato usually sold in North America as a yam.

## Method:

Peel the yam, grate coarsely and extract as much moisture as possible by squeezing in your hands.

In a large mixing bowl, mix the two flours with the baking powder, salt and turmeric. Toss in the grated yam.

Gradually add enough coconut milk to moisten. If the mixture becomes too dry, add more coconut milk; however, it should be solid enough to hold its shape.

In a large skillet, heat a tablespoon of the oil to medium-high heat. Lightly form a heaping teaspoon of the fritter mixture and fry on both sides until golden brown. Flatten slightly with a spatula to ensure the inside is cooked. You may need to add small amounts of oil as you go.

Once made, keep them in a warming dish in a preheated oven. Serve fritters with a plate of soft lettuce, herbs, bean sprouts and dipping sauces. **Yields 4 servings.**

# Greek Quesadillas

*What happens when Mexico heads for the Mediterranean?*
*A delicious and healthy combination of the old world and the new!*

### Ingredients:

| | | |
|---|---|---|
| 4 | **Whole grain tortillas** | 4 |
| 1 cup | Feta, crumbled | 250 ml |
| 1/2 cup | Hummus (see page 38) | 125 ml |
| 1/2 cup | Tzatziki (see page 44) | 125 ml |
| 1 cup | Kalamata olives, pitted & sliced | 250 ml |

### Method:

Preheat oven to 375°F. Prepare baking sheets.

Spread 2 tablespoons of hummus and tzatziki on each tortilla. Sprinkle 1/4 cup of cheese and olives on top of each tortilla and fold in half.

Place on a lined baking tray and bake 8-10 minutes or until golden and cheese is melted. Remove from oven and cool slightly before serving. Serve with extra tzatziki. **Yields 4 servings.**

# Maple-glazed Chicken Wings

*We really should call these "Canadian Wings" to distinguish them from the Buffalo Wings which originated in Buffalo, New York. Canada produces the best organic maple syrup in the world, and these chicken wings soar to new heights because of it!*

## Ingredients:

| | | |
|---|---|---|
| 2 lbs | Chicken wings, free-range or organic | 1 kg |
| 1/2 cup | Pure maple syrup | 125 ml |
| 1/4 cup | Grainy mustard | 60 ml |
| 2 tbsp | Tamari | 30 ml |
| 1 tbsp | Lemon juice | 15 ml |
| 2 tsp | Sea salt | 10 ml |
| 2 tsp | Chili flakes | 10 ml |

## Method:

Preheat oven to 375°F. Prepare a large baking sheet.

In a large bowl mix all ingredients (except the wings). Add in the wings and coat evenly.

Place on a baking tray and bake 20-25 minutes, turning often to glaze evenly. When golden brown and cooked (internal temperature of 170°F), remove from oven and enjoy hot. **Yields 4 servings.**

# Tuna-friendly Vegetarian Antipasto

*We're very pro-antipasto, and we promise you won't miss the fish in this tuna-free version. It will keep for 6 days in the fridge, but we've found that it rarely gets left alone that long!*

Ingredients:

| | | |
|---|---|---|
| 28 oz can | Whole tomatoes, drained and chopped | 796 g |
| 2 tbsp | Pickled peppers (hot or mild), finely chopped | 30 ml |
| 1/4 cup | Green pepper, diced | 60 ml |
| 1 cup | Carrots, diced | 250 ml |
| 1/4 cup | Kalamata olives, pitted and chopped | 60 ml |
| 1/4 cup | Green olives, pitted and chopped | 60 ml |
| 1 cup | Onions, diced | 250 ml |
| 1/2 cup | Celery, diced | 125 ml |
| 3 tbsp | Garlic, minced | 45 ml |
| 1/4 cup | Extra virgin olive oil | 60 ml |
| 2 tbsp | Apple cider vinegar | 30 ml |
| 1/2 tsp | Cumin, ground | 2 ml |
| 1/2 tsp | Sea salt | 2 ml |

Method:

Combine all ingredients except salt in a large pot. Bring to a boil, reduce heat to a simmer, stir often and cook 15-20 minutes until liquid is absorbed.

Remove from heat and season with salt. Cool. When cooled, place in a food processor or blender and blend until mixture is chopped but some texture still remains.

Serve chilled with your favourite crackers or as a dip for chips. Keeps refrigerated up to 6 days. **Yields 6 - 8 servings**.

# Tzatziki

*Homemade tzatziki is always better than pre-made, and tzatziki is good fresh but even better after the flavours have a chance to blend. It's light, low-fat and richly flavoured and a perfect match to the crunch of raw veggies. For best results, use full-fat yogurt – it still has much less fat than mayonnaise yet adds the necessary full body.*

## Tzatziki Fact
The base of this dip is yogurt, a great source of calcium and protein – calcium is needed in the body to help our bones and teeth grow.

## Ingredients:

| | | |
|---|---|---|
| 1 1/2 cups | Yogurt, full-fat | 750 ml |
| 1/2 tsp | Freshly ground black pepper | 2 ml |
| 1 1/2 tsp | Sea salt | 7 ml |
| 1 1/2 tsp | Parsley, dried | 7 ml |
| 1 1/2 tsp | Mint, fresh | 7 ml |
| 1/2 tsp | Dill, dried | 2 ml |
| 1 tbsp | Garlic, minced | 15 ml |
| 2 tbsp | Lemon juice | 30 ml |
| 1/2 | Cucumber, long English, seeded, grated and drained | 1/2 |

## Method:
Stir all ingredients in a bowl until well combined. **Yields 3 cups.**

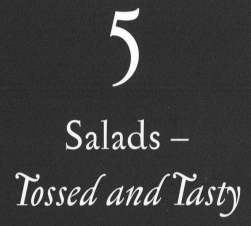

# 5
## Salads –
## *Tossed and Tasty*

Everyone has their own vision of salad. For some people, it's a wedge of iceberg lettuce and a glop of bottled Thousand Islands. For others, it's a fantastic concoction made with 12 kinds of greens, nuts, seeds, dried fruit, citrus and very little self-restraint. We prefer simple, but not too simple. Since a salad can start a meal, be the meal or finish a meal, we've included a range of our favourites suitable for all occasions.

PLANET
ORGANIC
M A R K E T

# 3-Minute Salads

*Sometimes people avoid salad because it seems time-consuming. Now they have no excuse – these are simple, delicious, fresh and, best of all, quick.*

## Organic Celery, Carrot and Caper Salad

| 4 | Celery stalks, finely chopped | 4 |
|---|---|---|
| 2 | Carrots, grated | 2 |
| 1 tbsp | Capers, drained | 15 ml |
| | Coleslaw dressing (see page 58) | |

**Method:**
Toss together with coleslaw dressing (see page 58).

## Orange, Red Onion and Kalamata Olive Salad

| 2 | Oranges | 2 |
|---|---|---|
| 1/2 cup | Red onion, cut into half moons | 125 ml |
| 6 - 9 | Kalamata olives, pitted and chopped | 6 - 9 |
| | Maple balsamic vinaigrette (see page 61) | |

**Method:**
With a paring knife, remove skin of 2 oranges. Remove all visible white pith. Slice oranges into slices across the grain. Toss with remaining ingredients and maple balsamic vinaigrette (see page 61).

## Spring Mix with Avocado and Toasted Pumpkin Seed Salad

| 1/2 cup | Pumpkin seeds | 125 ml |
|---|---|---|
| 5 oz | Spring mix salad | 150 g |
| 1 | Avocado, sliced into slim wedges | 1 |
| | Coleslaw dressing (see page 58) | |

**Method:**
In a small skillet, add the pumpkin seeds. Toast until the kernels make a popping sound. In a salad bowl, add spring mix, avocado and toasted pumpkin seeds and toss with coleslaw dressing (see page 58).

# ABC Six Bean Salad

*Each type of bean requires a different cooking time, which means you must cook each type of bean separately. That's what we do in our Planet kitchens, but you might want to choose 2 or 3 types of beans and just increase the volume so you end up with enough.*

## Ingredients:

| | | |
|---|---|---|
| 1/4 cup | Kidney beans, dry | 60 ml |
| 1/4 cup | Adzuki beans, dry | 60 ml |
| 1/2 cup | Black beans, dry | 125 ml |
| 1 cup | Chickpeas, dry | 250 ml |
| 1 cup | Mung beans, dry | 250 ml |
| 1 cup | Black eyed peas, dry | 250 ml |

## Dressing:

| | | |
|---|---|---|
| 1/4 cup | Fresh dill, chopped | 60 ml |
| 1 cup | Red pepper, diced | 250 ml |
| 1 cup | Yellow pepper, diced | 250 ml |
| 2 cloves | Garlic, minced | 2 cloves |
| 2 tsp | Sea salt | 30 ml |
| 1/3 cup | Red wine vinegar | 80 ml |
| 1/4 cup | Lemon juice | 60 ml |
| 1/4 cup | Extra virgin olive oil | 60 ml |
| 1/4 tsp | Freshly ground black pepper | 1 ml |

## Method:

See Bean *Appétit: Cooking with Beans* on page 148 for tips and techniques for cooking with beans.

Cook dried beans, drain, rinse with cool water. Mix together remaining ingredients separately. Add dressing to beans. **Yields 10 servings.**

# Hail-to-the-Kale Salad

*This salad is loaded with crunch. The combination of kale, carrots, cabbage and seeds makes a salad that is audibly delicious. Kale is extremely good for you, but make sure you chop it finely.*

Ingredients:

| | | |
|---|---|---|
| 1 bunch | Kale, chopped | 1 bunch |
| 3 cups | Carrots, grated | 750 ml |
| 1/2 head | Red cabbage, thinly sliced | 1/2 head |
| 1/2 cup | Tamari pumpkin seeds (see method below) | 125 ml |
| 1/2 cup | Tamari sunflower seeds (see method below) | 125 ml |
| 1/2 cup | Flax or hemp oil | 125 ml |
| 1/3 cup | Bragg Liquid Aminos | 80 ml |
| 5 tbsp | Balsamic vinegar | 75 ml |
| 1 tsp | Oregano, dried | 5 ml |

Method:

Wash kale and chop. Be careful to rinse the leaves to remove dirt and grit.

In a cast iron skillet over medium to high heat, stir sunflower and pumpkin seeds. Remove from heat when they're toasted golden brown. While the skillet is hot, add in a few drops of tamari, which will sear onto the seeds. Remove and let cool.

In a large bowl combine chopped kale, carrots, cabbage and seeds. Set aside.

In a small bowl whisk together oil, Bragg Liquid Aminos, vinegar and oregano and pour over kale mixture. Toss until evenly coated and chill 2 hours before serving. This salad keeps well refrigerated 2-3 days.
**Yields 8 - 10 servings.**

# Mediterranean Lentil Salad

*Green, red and yellow peppers add colour, character and extra nutrients to this earthy salad. Try French lentils – the tiny, dark green variety hold their shape and make the salad more appealing.*

### Ingredients:

| | | |
|---|---|---|
| 2 cups | French lentils | 500 ml |
| 1 cup | Fresh parsley, chopped | 250 ml |
| 1 tbsp | Garlic, minced | 15 ml |
| 1 cup | Green onion, thinly sliced | 250 ml |
| 1/4 cup | Sun-dried tomatoes, sliced | 60 ml |
| 1/4 cup | Extra virgin olive oil | 60 ml |
| 1/4 cup | Red wine vinegar | 60 ml |
| 2 tsp | Basil, dried | 10 ml |
| 1 cup | Yellow pepper, thinly sliced | 250 ml |
| 1 cup | Red pepper, thinly sliced | 250 ml |
| 1 cup | Green pepper, thinly sliced | 250 ml |
| 1 1/2 tsp | Sea salt | 7 ml |
| 1 tsp | Freshly ground black pepper | 5 ml |

### Method:

Bring a medium-sized pot of water to a boil, add lentils, reduce heat and cook until tender 20-30 minutes.

Remove from heat, drain and rinse under cold water to cool. Drain again and place in a large bowl. Add all remaining ingredients and toss to evenly coat.

May be refrigerated for up to 3 days. **Yields 6 - 8 servings.**

# Orzo Pasta Salad

*Pasta salad has a bad reputation – and deserves it. Tons of bland, starchy overcooked pasta with Italian dressing have put many of us off the stuff forever. With refreshing Mediterranean flavours and delicate orzo pasta, this is a pasta salad that will make you forget all that.*

## Ingredients:

| | | |
|---|---|---|
| 1 1/2 cup | Orzo pasta, dry | 625 ml |
| 1 - 2 tsp | Turmeric, ground | 5 - 10 ml |
| 1 tbsp | Extra virgin olive oil | 15 ml |
| 1/3 cup | Sun-dried tomatoes | 80 ml |
| 1 cup | Feta, crumbled | 250 ml |
| 1/3 cup | Capers, rinsed | 80 ml |
| 1/3 cup | Kalamata olives, pitted and chopped | 80 ml |
| 2 tbsp | Lemon juice | 30 ml |
| 1 tbsp | Garlic, minced | 15 ml |

## Method:

Bring a large pot of salted water to a boil and cook orzo pasta until al dente (7-10 minutes). Drain and rinse under cold water to cool. Drain again and place in a large bowl.

Toss with turmeric and oil until evenly coated. Add all remaining ingredients and mix until well combined.

*Note: Best served chilled. This salad keeps refrigerated 3-4 days and gets better as flavours develop.* **Yields 4 servings.**

# Roasted Veggie Salad

*Roasting makes even less-than-fresh veggies rich and delicious. A big bowl of roasted vegetables is unbelievably versatile – serve it on pizza, with pasta or in a wrap. And since any veggie roasts well, use your imagination – try beets, carrots, parsnips or baby onions.*

Ingredients:

| | | |
|---|---|---|
| 1 | Eggplant, diced | 1 |
| 2 cups | Zucchini, diced | 500 ml |
| 1 cup | Red onion, diced | 250 ml |
| 2 cups | Mushrooms, quartered | 500 ml |
| 1 cup | Red pepper, diced | 250 ml |
| 1 cup | Yellow pepper, diced | 250 ml |
| 1 cup | Green pepper, diced | 250 ml |
| 1/2 cup | Garlic, whole cloves | 125 ml |
| 3 tbsp | Extra virgin olive oil | 45 ml |
| 1/4 cup | Balsamic vinegar | 60 ml |
| 1/2 tsp | Sea salt | 2 ml |

Method:

Preheat oven to 375°F. In a large bowl, toss eggplant and zucchini with 1 tablespoon of the oil. Place on a baking sheet. In the same bowl, toss together onion, mushrooms, peppers, garlic and 2 tablespoons of oil. Place on a separate baking sheet.

Place both trays in oven and bake 20-25 minutes or until they are browned and garlic is soft, stirring twice to achieve even browning. Remove from oven and cool.

Place all veggies in a bowl and toss with vinegar and salt. Serve chilled or warmed.

*Note: Salad keeps well refrigerated 2-3 days.* **Yields 6 - 8 servings.**

# Sweet Potato Salad

*We call this "sweet potato" salad because our customers prefer the name, but it uses the moist-fleshed orange variant of sweet potatoes more commonly known as yams. That aside, this is a nicely updated and very healthy version of potato salad.*

**Sweet Potatoes**

Sweet potatoes (yams) are high in fibre, low in sodium and full of vitamins C, A and B6. Raisins and pecans add colour and texture, and the celery and red onion intensify the flavour.

## Ingredients:

| | | |
|---|---|---|
| 8 cups | Sweet potatoes (yams), peeled and cut into 1-inch cubes | 1.8 kg |
| 1 cup | Mayonnaise or vegan mayonnaise | 250 ml |
| 1/2 cup | Raisins | 125 ml |
| 1/2 cup | Pecans, unsalted and chopped | 125 ml |
| 3/4 tsp | Ginger, ground | 3 ml |
| 1/2 cup | Celery, 1/4-inch diced | 125 ml |
| 1/2 cup | Red onions, diced | 125 ml |
| 1/2 tsp | Sea salt | 2 ml |
| 1/2 tsp | Freshly ground black pepper | 2 ml |
| 2 tsp | Lemon juice | 10 ml |

## Method:

Steam potatoes until fork tender (about 20 minutes) then cool.

In a large bowl, combine all ingredients and toss gently with cooled, cooked potatoes. Chill in refrigerator before serving. **Yields 4 - 6 servings**.

# Yogurt Caesar Salad

**Cooking Tip**
Invest in a good salad spinner, it's the only way to remove dirt and grit and excess water from lettuce!

*Caesar salad is perhaps the most popular salad in the world. Our version solves the anchovy and raw egg concerns of Caesar fanatics. The yogurt and Dijon mustard replace the creaminess from eggs, and the balsamic vinegar stands in nicely for the Worcestershire sauce and/or anchovies. This makes for a nice, low-fat dressing and a very healthy version of a classic favourite.*

## Ingredients:

| | | |
|---|---|---|
| 1/3 cup | Plain yogurt, full-fat | 80 ml |
| 1 tbsp | Dijon mustard | 15 ml |
| 1 tbsp | Balsamic vinegar | 15 ml |
| 2 cloves | Garlic, minced | 2 cloves |
| 2 tbsp | Lemon juice | 30 ml |
| 1/2 tsp | Sea salt | 2 ml |
| 1/2 tsp | Freshly ground black pepper | 2 ml |
| 1 tbsp | Extra virgin olive oil | 15 ml |
| 1/2 tsp | Granulated cane sugar | 2 ml |
| 1/4 cup | Parmesan cheese, grated | 60 ml |
| 1 head | Romaine lettuce (washed and torn) | 1 head |

## Method:

In a medium-sized bowl, blend yogurt with mustard, balsamic vinegar and garlic. Add sugar, salt, pepper and lemon. Blend in 1 tablespoon of olive oil. Check consistency. If it seems too thick, add extra lemon juice.

It's important to let the dressing stand for at least 20 minutes to allow the flavours to meld. Taste carefully, adjust seasoning with lemon juice or salt.

Just before serving, stir in the Parmesan cheese. Have extra Parmesan cheese ready to sprinkle on top. Toss with washed, hand-torn romaine lettuce. **Yields 4 servings.**

# 6
# Dressings –
# *Impeccably Dressed*

At one time, in our fat-hating days, we might have been tempted by low-fat "lite" salad dressings full of synthetic emulsifiers and thickeners. Now we know that not all fats are equal, and that some – such as the organic canola and extra virgin olive oil in these recipes – are healthy. Even better, nutritionists now seem to agree that some fat in a meal helps us absorb more of the nutrients in vegetables. Pass the dressing!

PLANET
ORGANIC
MARKET

# Coleslaw Dressing

*Used with our Spinach Poppy-seed Salad (see page 6), this delicious dressing proves that it has a life far beyond coleslaw.*

Ingredients:

| | | |
|---|---|---|
| 1 tbsp | Brown mustard seeds, toasted | 15 ml |
| 1 cup | Mayonnaise | 250 ml |
| 2 tbsp | Apple cider vinegar | 30 ml |
| 1/4 cup | Pure honey | 60 ml |
| 1/4 tsp | Sea salt | 1 ml |
| 2 tbsp | Dijon mustard | 30 ml |

Method:

Whisk together all ingredients until well combined. Keep refrigerated until needed. Best if made a day ahead so flavours develop. **Yields 1 1/2 cups.**

# Everyday Orange Dressing

*A simple and tasty low-fat dressing. This tangy dressing is olive oil optional.*

## Ingredients:

| | | |
|---|---|---|
| 1/4 cup | Juice of 1 small orange or 1/2 of large orange | 60 ml |
| 1 tsp | Dijon mustard | 5 ml |
| 1 tbsp | Red wine or balsamic vinegar | 15 ml |
| 1 tbsp | Extra virgin olive oil (optional) | 15 ml |
| to taste | Sea salt | to taste |
| to taste | Freshly ground black pepper | to taste |

## Method:

In a small mixing bowl, add the dijon mustard. Blend in the orange juice slowly until smooth, adding vinegar, ensuring it is well blended.

Olive oil can be added here if preferred. Add a little sea salt and freshly ground black pepper. **Yields 2 servings**.

# Ginger Soy Dressing

*We sell a lot of bottles of this popular dressing, and it's easy to taste why. Tangy, salty, sweet — the mix of Asian flavours is rich and satisfying.*

**Variation:**
Add 1 tbsp of chopped, fermented black beans* to mixture.

* Available at Asian Markets

## Ingredients:

| | | |
|---|---|---|
| 2 tbsp | Canola oil | 30 ml |
| 2 tbsp | Toasted sesame oil | 30 ml |
| 1 tbsp | Ginger, minced | 15 ml |
| 1 tbsp | Garlic, minced | 15 ml |
| 2 cups | Tamari | 500 ml |
| 1 cup | Pure honey | 250 ml |
| dash | Anise, ground | dash |
| 1/4 cup | Water | 60 ml |
| 2 tbsp | Water | 30 ml |
| 1 tbsp | Cornstarch | 15 ml |

## Method:

In a medium pot, heat oils over medium heat and add garlic and ginger, cook 5 minutes.

Add tamari, honey, anise and first amount of water (1/4 cup). Bring to a boil, reduce heat and cook 10 minutes.

Whisk second amount (2 tablespoons) of water with cornstarch and slowly whisk into the hot sauce. Cook 2 minutes until sauce thickens. Remove from heat and cool completely.

*Note: Dressing keeps well for 3 weeks.* **Yields 3 cups.**

# Maple Balsamic Vinaigrette

*A tangy, sweet vinaigrette especially good for mixed green salads.*

## Ingredients:

| | | |
|---|---|---:|
| 5 - 6 tbsp | Balsamic vinegar | 75 - 90 ml |
| 2 tsp | Dijon mustard | 10 ml |
| 3 - 4 tbsp | Pure maple syrup | 45 - 60 ml |
| 1/2 cup | Extra virgin olive oil | 125 ml |
| 1/2 cup | Canola oil | 125 ml |
| to taste | Sea salt | to taste |
| to taste | Freshly ground black pepper | to taste |

## Method:

In a food processor or bowl, whisk the first 3 ingredients together, adding oil slowly at the end.

Taste to correct the balance of sweet and sour flavours, add more vinegar or maple syrup if needed. Store the vinaigrette in the refrigerator for several weeks. **Yields 1 1/4 cups.**

# Planet Organic Market Shallot Dressing

*Apple cider vinegar is an ancient food with many healthy attributes, but in this recipe we really just like the way it tastes!*

## Ingredients:

| | | |
|---|---|---|
| 1/4 cup | Red onion, diced | 60 ml |
| 1/4 cup | Shallots, diced | 60 ml |
| 2 tbsp | Dijon mustard | 30 ml |
| 1/3 cup | Apple cider vinegar | 80 ml |
| 1 tsp | Pure honey | 5 ml |
| 1 1/2 tsp | Sea salt | 7 ml |
| 1/2 tsp | Dill, dried | 2 ml |
| 1 cup | Canola oil | 250 ml |

## Method:

In a food processor or blender, combine all ingredients except oil until smooth.

Slowly add in oil while continuing to blend until it's incorporated and thickened. Keep refrigerated until needed. **Yields 1 3/4 cups.**

# Toasted Sesame Dressing

**Cooking Tip**

Miso comes in many different strengths. For a rich, intense flavour use Hatcho miso. For a milder flavour use Shiro (white) miso.

*This light and fresh-tasting dressing works beautifully with any Asian-inspired salad. Just make sure you have toasted sesame oil on hand.*

## Ingredients:

| | | |
|---|---|---|
| 3 tbsp | Sesame seeds | 45 g |
| 1/3 cup | Canola oil | 80 ml |
| 2 tbsp | Toasted sesame oil | 30 ml |
| 2 tbsp | Rice vinegar | 30 ml |
| 1 tbsp | Red miso | 15 ml |
| 2 cloves | Garlic | 2 cloves |
| 1/2 tsp | Sea salt | 2 ml |
| 1/2 cup | Water | 125 ml |

## Method:

Toast the sesame seeds in oven for 10 minutes at 300°F. In a blender or food processor mix with remaining ingredients. **Yields 3/4 cup.**

Beta-carotene Soup

Colour Me Healthy!
Vegetable Soup

Potato Provençal Soup

Spicy Pumpkin
Tofu Soup

Tomato Basil Soup

Vegetarian Split
Pea Soup

Vietnamese Chicken
Noodle Soup

# 7

## Soups –
### *Ladles of Love*

Are soups good for you? In 16th-century France, street vendors sold flavourful soups that were said to restore your energy called "restaurants." In 1765, the first retail outlet specializing in such soups opened in Paris and was named for its soup: the very first place known as a "restaurant." Soups are filling, usually easy and inexpensive to make, can often be frozen if needed and are an almost guaranteed source of leftovers. Restore yourself today: make some soup!

PLANET
ORGANIC
MARKET

# Beta-carotene Soup

*Orange you glad beta-carotene is so good for you? A great comfort food on a chilly winter day – this soup is filled with many different vegetables that are packed full of vitamin A and beta-carotene.*

*Connie DeKramer, our Edmonton cooking instructor, often inspires her class participants to try her macrobiotic favourites. This soup is chock full of nutritious root vegetables, and the kombu (seaweed) adds a rich undertone to the stock.*

> **Beta-carotene**
> Beta-carotene can be found in a variety of colourful vegetables, such as butternut squash, carrots and parsnips. This nutrient plays an important role in vision, immune defenses and bone growth.

## Ingredients:

| | | |
|---|---|---|
| 2 - 2 1/2 lbs | Butternut squash, peeled and cubed | 1 - 1.2 kg |
| 4 cups | Carrots, diced | 1 kg |
| 2 cups | Parsnips, diced | 500 ml |
| 1 cup | Onion, diced | 250 ml |
| 1 3-inch piece | Kombu seaweed | 1 3-inch piece |
| 1 tsp | Sea salt | 5 ml |
| 4 - 6 cups | Vegetable stock | 1 - 1.5 L |

## Method:

Place all ingredients in a large soup pot with enough stock to cover all the vegetables. Bring to a boil, reduce heat to a simmer and cook 45-60 minutes until vegetables are tender.

Remove from heat, remove kombu from mixture and cut into small pieces and return to pot. Using a potato masher, mash the vegetables until puréed. Serve hot. **Yields 4 servings.**

# Colour Me Healthy! Vegetable Soup

*When you visit the produce aisle, remember to fill your basket with vegetables from all the colours of the rainbow. The more colours you incorporate into your diet, the wider range of nutritional benefits you'll enjoy. Here's to a healthier, more colourful world!*

## Ingredients:

| | | |
|---|---|---|
| 1 cup | Onion, diced | 250 ml |
| 1 tbsp | Garlic, minced | 15 ml |
| 1 tbsp | Extra virgin olive oil | 15 ml |
| 1 cup | Carrot, grated | 250 ml |
| 1 cup | Parsnip, grated | 250 ml |
| 1 cup | Celery, diced | 250 ml |
| 1 cup | Broccoli, chopped | 250 ml |
| 1/2 cup | Green beans, diced | 125 ml |
| 28 oz can | Crushed tomatoes | 796 ml |
| 4 cups | Vegetable stock | 1 L |
| 2 tbsp | Oregano, dried | 30 ml |
| to taste | Sea salt | to taste |
| to taste | Freshly ground black pepper | to taste |

## Method:

In a large soup pot, heat oil and add onions and garlic. Cook over medium heat 3-5 minutes.

Add carrots, parsnips, celery, broccoli, beans, crushed tomatoes and stock and bring to a boil. Reduce heat to a simmer, add oregano and cook 15-20 minutes. Remove from heat and add salt and pepper to desired taste. **Yields 6 - 8 servings.**

# Potato Provençal Soup

*All the iconic flavours of southern France are in this soup —
leeks, tomatoes, basil and plenty of garlic.*

Ingredients:

| | | |
|---|---|---|
| 1 tbsp | Canola oil | 15 ml |
| 1 cup | Onion, diced | 250 ml |
| 3/4 cup | Red onion, diced | 180 ml |
| 1 cup | Celery, diced | 250 ml |
| 2 lbs | Yukon gold potatoes, diced | 1 kg |
| 1 tbsp | Garlic, minced | 15 ml |
| 1/2 cup | Fresh parsley, minced | 125 ml |
| 1/2 cup | Red peppers, diced | 125 ml |
| 1/4 cup | Leeks, dried | 60 ml |
| 14 oz can | Diced tomatoes | 400 g |
| 4 cups | Water | 1 L |
| 1/2 tsp | Basil, dried | 2 ml |
| 1/2 tsp | Thyme, dried | 2 ml |
| 1/2 tsp | Oregano, dried | 2 ml |
| 1 | Bay leaf | 1 |
| to taste | Sea salt | to taste |
| to taste | Freshly ground black pepper | to taste |

Method:

In a large soup pot, heat oil, add onions, celery, garlic, potatoes, peppers and leeks. Cook over medium heat 3-5 minutes.

Add tomatoes, herbs and water. Bring to a boil, reduce heat to a simmer and cook 15-20 minutes or until potatoes are tender. Season to taste with salt and pepper. **Yields 6 - 8 servings.**

# Spicy Pumpkin Tofu Soup

## Pumpkin

Superstar starches, including pumpkin and squash, pack a powerful antioxidant punch! These healthy veggies are high in beta-carotene to combat aging and protect the body from damaging free radicals.

## Cooking Tip

Use either pumpkin or squash in this recipe.

*Starchy soups are a fall tradition – perfect for warming up after an afternoon in the garden. We've spiced up a traditional recipe with red curry paste and coconut milk for a creamy alternative. Serve with a dollop of yogurt and green onions for a smart-looking soup.*

### Ingredients:

| | | |
|---|---|---|
| 1 tsp | Red curry paste | 5 ml |
| 14 oz can | Pumpkin purée | 400 g |
| 2 cups | Vegetable stock | 500 ml |
| 14 oz can | Coconut milk | 400 ml |
| 12 oz | Silken tofu, firm cubed | 340 g |
| 1/4 cup | Green onions, thinly sliced | 60 ml |
| 1/2 cup | Plain yogurt, full-fat (optional) | 125 ml |

### Method:

In a large soup pot, heat curry paste over medium heat until it starts to toast. Add pumpkin and stock and cook 5 minutes. Reduce heat to a simmer.

Add coconut milk and cubed tofu, stirring gently and cook until heated through. Serve with a dollop of yogurt and green onions sprinkled on top. **Yields 4 - 6 servings.**

# Tomato Basil Soup

*Ideally, you'll want to make this soup when fresh, vine-ripened tomatoes are in season, but what about the other 9 months of the year? Fortunately, soup made from organic canned tomatoes can be equally delicious.*

*An extra tip for those very hot summer days – this soup is excellent served cold, Gazpacho-style!*

**Cooking Tip**
Soup too acidic? Just add a small amount of honey or sugar to neutralize the acid.

## Ingredients:

| | | |
|---|---|---|
| 2 lbs or 28 oz can | Fresh tomatoes or whole tomatoes | 1 kg or 796 ml |
| 4 cups | Vegetable broth | 1 L |
| 1 tbsp | Granulated cane sugar | 15 ml |
| 1/4 cup | Fresh basil, chopped | 60 ml |
| 1/2 tsp | Sea salt | 2 ml |
| 1/8 tsp | Freshly ground black pepper | 1 ml |

## Method:

Chop tomatoes into large pieces. Place tomatoes in blender or food processor and blend until smooth.

Place puréed tomatoes in a soup pot with stock and sugar. Bring to a boil, reduce heat and simmer 10 minutes.

Remove from heat and add basil. Add salt and pepper to desired taste.
**Yields 4 servings.**

# Vegetarian Split Pea Soup

*This hearty classic combines green split peas, onions and carrots in a rich vegetable stock with a touch of garlic for that perfect flavour. Enjoy it on its own for a filling lunch or add fresh French bread and tossed salad for a lovely dinner.*

## Ingredients:

| | | |
|---|---|---|
| 2 tbsp | Extra virgin olive oil | 30 ml |
| 1 cup | Onion, diced | 250 ml |
| 2 tbsp | Garlic, minced | 30 ml |
| 2 cups | Carrots, diced | 500 ml |
| 2 cups | Green split peas, rinsed | 500 ml |
| 1 cup | Vegetable stock | 250 ml |
| 6 cups | Water | 1.5 L |
| 3 tbsp | Tomato paste | 45 ml |
| 1/2 tsp | Dill, dried | 2 ml |
| to taste | Sea salt | to taste |
| to taste | Freshly ground black pepper | to taste |

## Method:

In a large soup pot, heat oil over a medium heat. Add onions and garlic and cook over medium heat 5 minutes until golden brown.

Add carrots, peas, stock and water and bring to a boil. Reduce heat to a simmer and cook 30-45 minutes or until peas are tender and soft. Add remaining ingredients and stir until combined.

Remove from heat and cool slightly before processing with a hand wand, in a blender or food processor until smooth. **Yields 4 servings.**

# Vietnamese Chicken Noodle Soup

## Ingredients:

| | | |
|---|---|---|
| 4 cups | Chicken stock | 1 L |
| 4 cups | Water | 1 L |
| 1 tbsp | Fresh ginger, sliced | 15 ml |
| 1 | Cinnamon stick | 1 |
| 1/2 tsp | Coriander seed, whole | 2 ml |
| 3 | Star anise | 3 |
| 4 tsp | Fish sauce | 20 ml |
| 1 tsp | Granulated cane sugar | 5 ml |
| 1/2 tsp | Freshly ground black pepper | 2 ml |
| 8 | Shallots, thinly sliced | 8 |
| 1 tbsp | Canola oil (for frying) | 15 ml |
| 4 oz | Rice noodles | 110 g |
| 1/2 cup | Onion, thinly sliced | 125 ml |
| 4 oz | Chicken breast, chopped – free-range or organic | 110 g |
| 1 cup | Bean sprouts | 250 mg |
| 2 | Limes, quartered | 2 |
| 1/4 cup | Fresh cilantro, chopped | 60 ml |

*This fragrant soup stock is enriched with layers of Asian flavours, including star anise, coriander and cinnamon. It's a few extra steps, but well worth it!*

## Method:

In a large soup pot, bring chicken stock and water to a boil. Add ginger, cinnamon, coriander and star anise. Reduce and simmer for 15 minutes. Strain stock and remove spices. Return to heat and add fish sauce, sugar and pepper.

Meanwhile, pan-fry shallots until crispy. Drain and set aside.

Add chicken and onion to stock and simmer for 10 minutes. Minutes before serving, bring stock to boil and add rice noodles. Simmer until noodles are soft (6-8 minutes). Serve in large bowls with bean sprouts, quartered limes, chili sauce, chilies, cilantro and browned shallots. **Yields 8 servings.**

Mark Craft and Diane Shaskin purchase High Level Natural Foods and rename it *Terra Natural Food Market*. Terra introduces a "new look" to "health food stores", where the shopping experience itself is as important as the quality, selection and service.

Darren Krissie joins Mark and Diane in a plan to bring Terra style service, quality and ambience to natural food shopping across Canada. Darren pilots the new company, called Planet Organic Health Corp, onto the Canadian Venture Exchange.

Braised Beef with
Mushrooms and Barley

Goat Cheese
Stuffed Meatloaf

Mango Sesame Chicken

Organic Tuscan Beef

Chicken and
Chickpea Chili

Asian-Influenced
Red Chili Fish

Roast Italian-style
Free-range Chicken

# 8
# Poultry, Beef and Fish Main Dishes –
## *Our Cows Don't Do Drugs*

There has never been a better time to be a carnivore. Healthy, wild fish, free-range and organic poultry and organic beef have never been more widely available. And that's not only better for cooks and food lovers, it's better and healthier for the animals and the planet we share with them. Now that you have the choice, why wouldn't you choose wild or organic?

PLANET
ORGANIC
M A R K E T

# Braised Beef with Mushrooms and Barley

*Combined with barley, braised beef makes a homey, nutritious comfort dish that is welcome in the cool winter months.*

Ingredients:

| | | |
|---|---|---|
| 1 tbsp | Canola oil | 15 ml |
| 3 lbs | Blade or round beef, chunks, organic | 1.5 kg |
| 1 lb | Mushrooms, quartered | 500 g |
| 1 cup | Onion, diced | 250 ml |
| 3 tbsp | Garlic, minced | 45 ml |
| 1 1/4 cup | Beef broth | 310 ml |
| 1/2 cup | Pearl barley | 125 ml |
| 1 | Bay leaf | 1 |
| 1 tsp | Sea salt | 5 ml |
| 1/4 tsp | Freshly ground black pepper | 1 ml |
| 1 cup | Fresh or frozen peas | 250 ml |
| 1/3 cup | Sour cream (optional) | 80 ml |

**Braising**

Braising is a wonderful and ancient way to transform any cut of meat into a tender, richly flavoured meal.

Method:

Preheat oven to 325°F. Heat oil in a large skillet until hot (over medium heat). Add beef chunks and brown until golden (about 3 minutes...don't crowd the pan). Remove from pan and place in an ovenproof baking pan.

In frying pan with beef drippings, add mushrooms, onions and garlic and cook 3-5 minutes. Sprinkle over top of beef. Add broth to frying pan and bring to a boil. Pour over beef, add bay leaf, salt and pepper and place in oven. Cook 30 minutes. Add barley and cover with foil. Continue to bake 45-60 minutes until barley is tender. Remove from oven, remove bay leaf. Stir in peas and sour cream, if desired. Serve hot. **Yields 4 - 6 servings.**

# Goat Cheese Stuffed Meatloaf

*Perhaps the ultimate East meets West fusion recipe, this meatloaf dish was inspired by a sushi roll. By rolling the ground meat around a layer of goat cheese like a jelly roll, the cheese is layered into the centre of the meatloaf.*

Ingredients:

| | | |
|---|---|---|
| 1 lb | Ground beef, organic | 500 g |
| 1/2 cup | Bread crumbs | 125 ml |
| 1 | Egg | 1 |
| 1/4 cup | Onion, chopped | 60 ml |
| 1 tbsp | Worcestershire sauce | 15 ml |
| 1/2 tsp | Sea salt | 2 ml |
| 1 tbsp | Dijon mustard | 15 ml |
| 1 pkg | Goat cheese round, plain | 100 g |
| 1 tbsp | Butter, softened | 15 ml |
| 2 tbsp | Ketchup or tomato paste | 30 ml |

Method:

Preheat oven to 350°F. Prepare a 9"x 5" loaf pan.

Mix all ingredients together (except for butter and ketchup or tomato paste). Do not over mix. Pat meat mixture into a rectangle (about 10" square) on a piece of plastic wrap or aluminum foil. To prepare goat cheese, put into a small bowl and mix into a smooth paste with 1 tablespoon of butter. Spread the goat cheese mixture across the top of the meat in a neat stripe (about 3" from the top).

Roll like a giant sushi roll (don't get the foil caught in the roll!). Gently place in a casserole dish. Mix butter and ketchup or tomato paste together and spread a thin layer on top of the loaf. Bake at 350°F for about 45 minutes to 1 hour until done. **Yields 6 servings**.

# Mango Sesame Chicken

Ingredients:

| | | |
|---|---|---|
| 1/2 cup | Plain yogurt, full-fat | 125 ml |
| 1/3 cup | Mango chutney | 80 ml |
| 2 tbsp | Fresh cilantro, chopped | 30 ml |
| 4 single | Chicken breasts, free-range or organic (skin removed) | 4 single |
| 1/2 cup | Lemon juice | 125 ml |
| 3/4 cup | Sesame seeds | 180 ml |
| 4 cloves | Garlic, minced | 4 cloves |
| 4 tbsp | Curry powder | 60 ml |
| to taste | Sea salt | to taste |
| to taste | Freshly ground black pepper | to taste |

*The nutty coating for this chicken is perfectly matched with the cool, tangy smoothness of the yogurt and mango dip. Although curry and chutney are used, it's not too spicy.*

**Method:**

Preheat oven to 400°F. Lightly grease baking sheet.

In a small bowl, blend chutney, yogurt and cilantro. Cover and chill. Arrange chicken breasts in a shallow non-reactive dish (pound them lightly first). Pour lemon juice over them and marinate for 15-30 minutes. Drain chicken.

In a small bowl, combine sesame seeds, garlic, curry powder, salt and pepper. Spread garlic/curry mixture onto a dinner plate. Press chicken into sesame seed mixture, coating completely on both sides. Carefully put coated chicken onto baking tray and bake until just cooked (about 20 minutes).

Remove from oven and let stand 10 minutes (allows juices to settle and coating to solidify). Cut chicken crosswise into 1/2-inch strips. Place chicken strips on platter, decorate with fresh parsley. Serve with mango/yogurt sauce as a dipping sauce. **Yields 4 servings.**

## Cooking Tip

Many chutneys have big chunks of mango in them. For a smoother sauce, put chutney through a food processor or blender before adding the yogurt.

# Organic Tuscan Beef

*Once difficult to find, organic beef is now readily available in all our markets.*

## Ingredients:

| | | |
|---|---|---|
| 4 | Rib eye or sirloin steaks, organic | 4 |
| 1/2 cup | Extra virgin olive oil | 125 ml |
| 3 tbsp | Balsamic vinegar | 45 ml |
| 2 tbsp | Rosemary, dried or fresh | 30 ml |
| 1 tsp | Oregano, dried or fresh | 5 ml |
| 2 tbsp | Garlic, minced | 30 ml |
| to taste | Sea salt | to taste |
| to taste | Freshly ground black pepper | to taste |

## Method:

In a blender, combine all wet and dry ingredients until well blended.

Place steaks in a large pan and top with half of marinade. Flip steaks and top with remaining half. Refrigerate 2 hours or overnight.

When ready to cook, preheat oven to 400°F or preheat grill. If oven baking, place on a baking tray and cook 7-10 minutes on each side depending on desired level of doneness. If grilling, place on grill and cook each side 3-5 minutes, depending on desired level of doneness. Serve hot. **Yields 4 servings.**

# Chicken and Chickpea Chili

*If you want comfort food in a hurry, this is a simple recipe that provides a healthy and filling chili – in about half an hour.*

## Ingredients:

| | | |
|---|---|---|
| 1 lb | Ground chicken or turkey, free-range or organic | 500 g |
| 2 tbsp | Canola oil | 30 ml |
| 1 cup | Onions, diced | 250 ml |
| 3 tbsp | Garlic, minced | 45 ml |
| 28 oz can | Crushed tomatoes | 796 ml |
| 19 oz can | Chickpeas, cooked | 540 ml |
| 1 cup | Green pepper, diced | 250 ml |
| 2 tsp | Chili powder | 10 ml |
| 1 tsp | Cumin, ground | 5 ml |
| 2 tsp | Sea salt | 10 ml |
| 1/4 tsp | Freshly ground black pepper | 1 ml |
| 1/4 cup | Fresh cilantro, chopped (optional) | 60 ml |

### Chickpeas

Chickpeas have a nutty flavour and are high in fibre and are low-fat – a combination that is healthy for your heart. Foods high in fibre, such as chickpeas, are associated with lowering blood cholesterol and decreasing the risk of heart disease.

### Cooking Tip

Chili keeps refrigerated 4-5 days and actually tastes better on the second day.

## Method:

In a large, heavy-bottomed sauce pan or Dutch oven over medium heat, brown chicken with canola oil until cooked through. Add onions and garlic and cook 3-5 minutes.

Add remaining ingredients except cilantro and bring to a boil. Reduce heat and simmer 20-25 minutes until flavours have developed. Remove from heat and serve hot. Sprinkle with cilantro if desired. **Yields 4 servings.**

# Asian-influenced Red Chili Fish

*The mild flavour of white fish such as cod, haddock or halibut is a nice counterpart to the spicy Asian-influenced flavours of this beautiful dish.*

## Ingredients:

| | | |
|---|---|---|
| 2 | Red chili peppers, dried | 2 |
| 3/4 cup | Brown sugar | 175 ml |
| 1 tsp | Garlic, minced | 5 ml |
| pinch | Oregano, dried | pinch |
| 1/2 tsp | Sea salt | 2 ml |
| 2 tbsp | Lime juice | 30 ml |
| 2 tbsp | Canola oil | 30 ml |
| 2 lbs | Filet of halibut, or any white fish (haddock, cod, halibut, etc.) | 1 kg |
| 1 | Lime, thinly sliced | 1 |

## Method:

Preheat oven to 400°F. In a small bowl, place the dried peppers and cover with hot water. Let sit 15 minutes or until soft. Remove stem and seeds from pepper.

Put pepper, sugar, garlic, oregano, salt, lime juice and oil in a blender and blend to form a paste. Add extra water a tablespoon at a time to thin if needed. Spread paste over top side of fish, then place lime slices on top.

Place on a baking tray and bake at 400°F for 8-10 minutes or until cooked (depends on thickness and kind of fish used). Check fish with a knife; if it flakes then it's done. Remove from oven and serve hot. **Yields 4 servings**.

# Roast Italian-style Free-range Chicken

## Ingredients:

| | | |
|---|---|---|
| 4 - 5 lbs | Whole roasting chicken, free-range or organic | 2.2 kg |
| 4 - 6 | Yukon gold potatoes | 4 - 6 |
| 1 - 2 | Onion, cut into chunks | 1 - 2 |
| 1/4 cup | Extra virgin olive oil | 60 ml |
| 2 tbsp | Whole Italian spices (found at Planet Organic Market) | 30 ml |
| 1 tbsp | Coarse sea salt | 15 ml |
| 2 tbsp | Capers, drained | 30 ml |
| 1/3 cup | Lemon juice (reserve lemon rind) | 80 ml |
| 8 or more cloves | Garlic, whole and unpeeled | 8 or more cloves |

*Roast chicken the easy way: no basting, no bother. The result is a very tender roast chicken with crisp, delectable skin – and a delicious pan of roasted vegetables. Don't be afraid of the high heat – it's the secret ingredient.*

## Method:

Preheat oven to 400°F. Wash and pat dry chicken. Mix salt and spices and rub inside of chicken. Put reserved lemon rinds in cavity. Rub olive oil on outside, rub on spice/salt mixture. Place on rack in roasting pan with breast side up with wings folded under. Squeeze 1/3 cup of lemon juice over chicken and put into heated oven.

Meanwhile, wash and clean potatoes in cold water and cut into eighths. Toss potatoes, onion and garlic in olive oil. Set aside. Let chicken roast for 45 minutes before adding potatoes, onions and garlic to the bottom of the pan; 15 minutes later, add the capers. Check for doneness with a meat thermometer (poultry should reach 180°F in the thickest part of the thigh) at total roasting time of 1 hour and 30 minutes.

Place chicken on platter and cover with foil. Chicken skin will be dark and crispy. Let the chicken rest until ready to slice and serve. Meanwhile, stir the vegetables and continue cooking until they are done. **Yields 4 - 6 servings.**

### Cooking Tip

Invest in a roasting pan with an insert rack. This allows the drippings to fall away from the chicken, instead of it cooking in its own juices.

PLANET
ORGANIC
MARKET

# 9
# Vegetarian
# Main Dishes –
# *Power to the Peapod!*

Whether we choose meat-free eating as a way of life or just to add variety to our diet, vegetarian cooking has a strong tradition in almost every great world cuisine. Pasta, Dal, Asian noodles, even chili – these recipes exemplify the amazing variety of wonderful flavours, textures and styles available without animal protein. Vegetables shouldn't always be relegated to side dishes – they're ready to take centre stage!

# Buckwheat Noodles with Spicy Peanut Sauce

*Soba, Japanese buckwheat noodles, although historically associated with the Tokyo region, are now found throughout Japan everywhere from train station food stalls to fine restaurants. The spicy peanut sauce – using un-Japanese peanut butter – is a delicious way to enjoy these healthy noodles.*

## Ingredients:

| | | |
|---|---|---|
| 16 oz | Soba noodles, buckwheat | 500 g |
| 2 tbsp | Toasted sesame oil | 30 ml |
| 1/2 cup | Fresh cilantro, chopped | 125 ml |
| 1/4 cup | Scallions, chopped | 60 ml |
| 12 oz | Tofu, firm or golden (see page 88), cut into small cubes | 340 g |
| | Spicy peanut sauce (see page 87) | |
| 2 tbsp | Roasted unsalted peanuts, chopped or toasted black sesame seeds | 30 ml |
| | Fresh cilantro sprigs for garnish | |

## Method:

Bring a large pot of water to boil for the noodles. Meanwhile, in a small bowl, mix together the oil, cilantro, scallions and tofu. When the water boils, add salt to taste and the noodles. Cook until the noodles are just done (about 6 minutes).

Immediately dump them into a colander and rinse them with cold water to stop the cooking process. Shake off the excess water, then toss the noodles with tofu/oil mixture. Cover and refrigerate until ready to use, then toss with the peanut sauce. Garnish with the roasted peanuts or sesame seeds and fresh cilantro sprigs. **Yields 4 - 6 servings.**

### Buckwheat

Buckwheat is unrelated to wheat. Rich in selenium and zinc and other nutrients, it's a gluten-free grain from a plant related to rhubarb that is a good alternative for those with wheat or gluten sensitivity.

### Variation

If you prefer to have the noodles hot, shake off the excess water when they're finished cooking, but don't rinse them. Warm the sauce over a double boiler and toss it with the noodles.

# Spicy Peanut Sauce

Ingredients:

| | | |
|---|---|---|
| 2 cloves | Garlic, minced<br>(more if you are a garlic-lover) | 2 cloves |
| 1/2 cup | Fresh cilantro, leaves and<br>upper stems only | 125 ml |
| 2 tbsp | Fresh ginger, peeled<br>and roughly chopped | 30 ml |
| 2 tbsp | Toasted sesame oil | 30 ml |
| 1 tbsp | Canola oil | 15 ml |
| 1/2 cup | Natural peanut butter | 125 ml |
| 1/2 cup | Tamari | 125 ml |
| 3 tbsp | Brown sugar | 45 ml |
| 1/2 tsp | Red pepper flakes | 2 ml |
| 3 tbsp | Brown rice wine vinegar | 45 ml |
| | Hot water (if necessary) | |

Method:

Put the garlic, cilantro, red pepper flakes and ginger in a food processor and work until they are finely chopped. Add the oils, peanut butter, tamari and sugar; process again until well combined with the seasonings.

Stop and scrape down the sides once or twice. Add the vinegar and season to taste with additional tamari, if necessary. If the sauce is thicker than you wish, thin it with hot water.

Store the sauce in an airtight jar and keep it refrigerated. Thin it again with hot water as needed before using. *Note: If covered and refrigerated, it will keep for months*. **Yields 1 1/2 cups.**

# Golden Tofu

*This recipe not only tastes great, it will also cure any thoughts that all tofu is bland mush. These fried tofu cubes can be enjoyed on their own with any sauce you like, as the star of a stir-fry, atop a bed of greens or rice, or as a healthy substitute for croutons or chicken on a salad.*

### Ingredients:

| | | |
|---|---|---|
| 1 lb | Tofu, firm, cut into 3/4-inch cubes | 500 g |
| 1 tbsp | Canola oil | 15 ml |
| pinch | Sea salt | pinch |

### Cooking Tip

If you're using medium-firm tofu, the extra moisture has to be removed first. Put the tofu on a dinner plate and then place a cutting board on top with a small can on top, (for weight). Let the extra water be expressed out of the tofu before you move to the next steps.

### Method:

Drain the tofu and cut into cubes.

Heat the oil in a medium nonstick skillet over fairly high heat. Add the tofu and fry until golden.

It takes several minutes to colour, so let it cook undisturbed, then come back and gently turn the pieces. While they should brown, don't let them get dry and hard. Drain briefly on paper towels, then slide onto a heated serving dish and salt lightly. **Yields 9 servings.**

# Kamut Rotini with Fresh Tomatoes, Avocado and Basil

*This light and flavourful pasta, along with a combination of tomatoes, avocado and basil, will lift your spirits.*

### Avocado

Avocados add a creamy texture, as well as providing monounsaturated fat. Even better, they help the body absorb fat-soluble nutrients such as alpha- and beta-carotene and lutein.

### Variation

While pasta is cooking, steam zucchini and firm tofu (chopped into mall cubes). Add to sauce.

## Ingredients:

| | | |
|---|---|---|
| 1 lb | Fresh tomatoes, ripe | 500 g |
| 2 cloves | Garlic, minced | 2 cloves |
| 3 tbsp | Extra virgin olive oil | 45 ml |
| 1/4 cup | Fresh basil, hand-torn | 60 ml |
| 1 tbsp | Balsamic vinegar | 15 ml |
| to taste | Sea salt | to taste |
| to taste | Freshly ground black pepper | to taste |
| 1 | Avocado, medium ripe | 1 |
| 12 oz | Kamut rotini | 340 g |

## Method:

In a large pot, bring plenty of water to a boil. Drop the tomatoes into the boiling pasta water for about 30 seconds. Use a slotted spoon to remove them.

Place them in a bowl of cool water, making the tomatoes easier to peel, core, seed and chop. These extra steps are the secret to this great tasting no-cook sauce. Place chopped tomatoes in a bowl large enough to hold sauce and cooked pasta.

Add garlic, oil, basil, vinegar, salt and pepper to taste and mix gently (sauce should be covered and set aside for at least 10 minutes and up to an hour).

Just before serving, peel, pit and cut avocado into 1/2-inch cubes. Add to bowl with tomatoes. Use the same water that you prepped the tomatoes in to cook the pasta until al dente. Drain and toss to blend with sauce. Divide pasta among four plates and serve immediately. **Yields 4 servings**.

# Mediterranean Chickpea Stew

## Ingredients:

| | | |
|---|---|---|
| 2 | Leeks (or one large onion) | 2 |
| 1 tbsp | Lemon juice and zest of one lemon | 15 ml |
| 2 tbsp | Extra virgin olive oil | 30 ml |
| 1 1/2 tsp | Coriander, ground | 7 ml |
| 1 tsp | Cumin, ground | 5 ml |
| 1 tsp | Fennel seed, ground | 5 ml |
| 1/2 tsp | Sea salt | 2 ml |
| 1/8 tsp | Cayenne pepper | .5 ml |
| 14 oz can | Diced tomatoes, with their juices | 398 ml |
| 14 oz can | Chickpeas, rinsed and drained | 398 ml |
| 12 | Kalamata olives, pitted and chopped | 12 |
| | Pita bread, hot, cooked millet or basmati rice | |
| 1 - 2 oz | Feta cheese, broken into small pieces | 25 - 50 g |

*This stew brings together the classic ingredients of Mediterranean cooking to create an easy and satisfying dish that can be made in less than 30 minutes in one skillet!*

## Method:

Trim the leeks, slit them lengthwise in half and rinse well under running water to remove any sand or grit. Coarsely chop the leeks or onions.

Grate the zest from the organic lemon and squeeze 1 tablespoon of juice from half of the same lemon; set aside. In a large skillet, heat the oil over medium heat. Add the leeks (or onions), coriander, cumin, fennel, salt and cayenne. Cook, stirring often, until the leeks (or onions) are soft, about 5 minutes. Add the tomatoes with their liquid, the chickpeas, olives and lemon zest. Bring to a boil.

Reduce the heat to medium and cook, stirring occasionally, until the tomato sauce is very thick, about 15 minutes. Remove from the heat and stir in the lemon juice. Serve immediately over cooked millet, rice or pita bread. Garnish with feta cheese. **Yields 4 servings.**

# Lentil Loaf with Mashed Potatoes

*This is the holiday main course most recommended by turkeys. The flavours are reminiscent of classic turkey stuffing, but it's completely vegan – including the delicious herbed gravy.*

## Ingredients:

| | | |
|---|---|---|
| 1/2 cup | Green lentils (not red), rinsed | 125 ml |
| 1 1/2 cups | Long grain rice, cooked | 375 ml |
| 2 cloves | Garlic, minced | 2 cloves |
| 2 1/2 cups | Water or vegetable broth | 625 ml |
| 3/4 tsp | Sea salt | 3 ml |
| 2 tsp | Basil, dried | 10 ml |
| 2 tsp | Parsley, dried | 10 ml |
| 1 | Red onion, finely chopped | 1 |
| 1 | Celery stalk, thinly sliced | 1 |
| 1 | Carrot, thinly sliced or diced | 1 |
| 1 cup | Bread crumbs | 250 ml |
| 1 tbsp | Dijon mustard | 15 ml |
| 1 - 2 | Eggs, lightly beaten (optional) | 1 - 2 |
| | Mashed Potatoes (see page 92) | |
| | Herbed Gravy (see page 93) | |

## Method:

Preheat oven to 350°F. Lightly oil a 9"x 5" loaf pan.

In medium saucepan, place lentils and vegetable broth (or water) and bring to a full boil. Reduce heat, cover and simmer for 30 minutes. Add 3/4 teaspoon of salt, then continue simmering for about 15 minutes or until lentils are soft and the water has been absorbed.

In a medium-sized skillet, sauté onions and garlic in oil until translucent. Add celery and carrots, cover and cook for 5 minutes. Pour cooked vegetables into a large mixing bowl and combine with bread crumbs, rice, lentils, seasonings and eggs (if using); mix well. Place mixture in loaf pan. Spread a thick layer of Mashed Potatoes (see page 92) on top. Bake uncovered for 30 minutes. Serve with Herbed Gravy (see page 93). **Yields 6 servings.**

# Mashed Potatoes

## Ingredients:

| 2 lbs | Yukon gold potatoes | 1 kg |
|---|---|---|
| to taste | Sea salt | to taste |
| to taste | Freshly ground black pepper | to taste |

## Method:

Boil potatoes for 20 minutes or until done. Drain potatoes, reserve 1 cup of the cooking liquid.

Mash potatoes, adding 1/2 cup of liquid. Season with salt and pepper. Add more liquid if necessary. **Yields enough for a generous, thick layer on top of the lentil loaf.**

# Herbed Gravy

**Variation**

**Mushroom Gravy**
Add sautéd mushrooms
and onions when gravy
is simmering. Eliminate
herbs and adjust other
seasonings to taste.

## Ingredients:

| | | |
|---|---|---|
| 1/3 cup | Whole wheat pastry flour | 80 ml |
| 1 cup | Rice milk, original flavour | 250 ml |
| 1 tbsp | Tamari | 15 ml |
| 1 cup | Water | 250 ml |
| 1/2 tsp | Sea salt | 2 ml |
| 2 tbsp | Canola or safflower oil | 30 ml |
| 1 tsp | Sage, dried and crushed | 5 ml |
| 1/4 tsp | Thyme, dried | 1 ml |
| 1/4 tsp | Marjoram, dried | 1 ml |
| to taste | Freshly ground black pepper | to taste |

## Method:

In a large saucepan, heat oil over medium heat. Add flour and stir often for 2 minutes. Remove from heat and allow to cool for several minutes.

In a separate bowl, combine remaining ingredients.

Whisk together with the flour/oil, half at a time to avoid lumping. Bring to boil over medium heat, stirring often. Reduce heat to low and cook for 10-15 minutes, stirring occasionally. If gravy seems too thick, simply whisk in additional water, 1 tablespoon at a time until desired consistency is reached. Adjust salt and pepper to taste. Gravy will thicken as it cools.

Stores well in the refrigerator for several days. To serve at a later time, reheat slowly over medium heat, making sure to stir well. Add a tablespoon or two of water if necessary. **Yields 1 1/2 - 2 cups.**

# Potato Vegetable Curry

### Ingredients:

| | | |
|---|---|---|
| 3 tbsp | Canola oil | 45 ml |
| 1 tbsp | Yellow mustard seeds | 15 ml |
| 1 1/2 tsp | Cumin seeds | 7 ml |
| 3/4 cup | Red onion, diced | 180 ml |
| 1 - 3 tbsp | Ginger, minced | 15 - 45 ml |
| 1 tbsp | Garlic, minced | 15 ml |
| 1 tsp | Coriander, ground | 5 ml |
| 1/2 - 1 tsp | Garam Masala (or curry) | 2 - 5 ml |
| 2 tsp | Turmeric | 10 ml |
| 1/2 - 1 tsp | Cayenne Pepper | 2 - 5 ml |
| 4 cups | Potatoes, cubed | 1 kg |
| 1 cup | Carrots, diced | 250 ml |
| 2 cups | Cauliflower, florets | 500 ml |
| up to 1 cup | Water | up to 250 ml |
| 1 cup | Peas, fresh | 250 ml |
| 1/2 tsp | Sea salt | 5 ml |

*Thanks to Jasjit Singh, our cooking instructor who helped perfect this recipe for an authentic curry.*

### Variation
If you prefer a mild version, use only 1/2 teaspoon each of cayenne pepper and Garam Masala and 1 tablespoon of ginger.

### Method:
Preheat oven to 400°F. In a large bowl, combine potatoes, cauliflower and carrots. Toss with 1 tablespoon of oil, ensuring that all the vegetables are coated with oil.

On a baking sheet, place vegetables and roast for about 40 minutes, stirring every 15 minutes, until potatoes are done.

While the vegetables are roasting, heat 2 tablespoons of oil in a large pan. When hot, add mustard and cumin seeds and cook until the seeds start to pop, about 2 minutes.

Add onion and cook until caramelized. Add ginger and garlic and cook a few minutes. Then add spices, stir slowly, adding water a little at a time. Add roasted vegetables and peas. Cook until the vegetables are well coated. Garnish with fresh cilantro and serve. **Yields 6 servings.**

# Sweet Potato-topped Shepherd's Pie

*This is a delicious, sheep-friendly version of shepherd's pie – perfect for all those vegetarian shepherds and shepherdesses.*

### Cooking Tip

The vegetarian ground round doesn't need to be cooked, just heated through.

## Ingredients:

| | | |
|---|---|---|
| 3 lbs | Sweet potatoes, cubed | 1.5 kg |
| 1/4 cup | Butter | 60 ml |
| 1/4 cup | Whole milk | 60 ml |
| to taste | Sea salt | to taste |
| 1 tsp | Freshly ground black pepper | 5 ml |
| 2 cups | Corn or peas (fresh or frozen) | 500 ml |
| 2 tbsp | Canola oil | 30 ml |
| 1 1/2 lbs | Vegetarian ground round | 750 g |
| 1/4 cup | Onion, diced | 60 ml |
| 2 tbsp | Garlic, minced | 30 ml |
| 2 tbsp | Unbleached white flour | 30 ml |
| 1/2 cup | Water | 125 ml |

## Method:

Preheat oven to 350°F. Prepare 9" square, deep-sided baking pan or a 9" x 13" baking dish.

Place sweet potatoes in a large pot and cover with water. Bring to a boil, reduce heat and cook 15-20 minutes or until tender. Drain and mash together with butter, milk, salt and pepper. Set aside.

In a large skillet, add oil and heat over medium heat. Add onions and garlic and cook 3-5 minutes. Add vegetarian ground round and cook 1 minute. Sprinkle flour onto mixture and stir. Increase heat to medium-high and add water. Cook 3-5 minutes until boiling and sauce thickens. Pour mixture into baking pan. Top with corn (or peas), then mashed potatoes, spreading evenly. Cover with foil and bake 20-25 minutes or until heated through. Remove from oven and serve hot.
**Yields 4 - 6 servings.**

# The Best Dal Ever

### Ingredients:

| | | |
|---|---|---|
| 1 1/2 cups | Yellow split peas (chana dal) | 375 ml |
| 4 cups | Water | 1 L |
| 1 1/2 tsp | Sea salt | 7 ml |
| 1 tsp | Turmeric | 5 ml |
| 3 tbsp | Butter | 45 ml |
| 1 cup | Red onion, diced | 250 ml |
| 1 tsp | Cumin seeds | 5 ml |
| 1/2-inch | Cinnamon stick | 1/2-inch |
| 1/4 tsp | Cayenne | 1 ml |
| 1 tsp | Fresh ginger, finely grated | 5 ml |
| 1/4 tsp | Coriander, ground | 1 ml |
| 1/2 tsp | Garam Masala (or curry) | 2 ml |
| 1 - 2 | Cloves, crushed | 1 - 2 |
| | Fresh cilantro, leaves | |

*Dal, the ultimate Indian comfort food, is made hundreds of different ways with dozens of kinds of lentils. But since it's our cookbook, we get to pick favourites — hence the name!*

### Method:

Rinse the peas carefully to remove dirt and debris. Place rinsed peas, water, turmeric and salt in a large pot and bring to a boil. Reduce heat and cook until peas are a soft purée and most of the water is absorbed. Add more water if required. Be sure to stir often as peas will tend to stick to the bottom of the pot.

In frying pan, heat butter; add cumin seeds and chopped red onion and fry until caramelized. Add the ginger, and spices and cook until you see separation of oil on the side of the pan. Add to peas and mix well. Garnish with cilantro leaves.

Serve right away as peas will tend to thicken as they sit. Serve over basmati rice with hot, fresh, buttered naan or pita bread on the side. **Yields 4 - 6 servings.**

# Vegetarian Black Bean Chili

**TVP**

TVP (textured vegetable protein) is an original health food! This second-generation soy product contains 70% protein and is low in fat – it has been an essential in vegetarian cooking for decades.

*This classic has been a favourite at Planet Organic Market for 15 years! It's easy to make and has just enough spice and kick for everyone's taste buds. The textured soy protein adds extra protein and gives the chili a meaty texture.*

Ingredients:

| | | |
|---|---|---|
| 3 cups dried or 3 - 19 oz cans | Black beans, dried or canned | 750 ml or 3 - 540 ml cans |
| 6 cloves | Garlic, crushed | 6 cloves |
| 3 tsp | Cumin, ground | 15 ml |
| 2 1/4 tsp | Sea salt | 12 ml |
| 2 tsp | Basil, dried | 10 ml |
| 1 1/2 tbsp | Chili powder | 20 ml |
| 1 tsp | Oregano, dried | 5 ml |
| 1/4 tsp | Cayenne pepper | 1 ml |
| to taste | Freshly ground black pepper | to taste |
| 2 tbsp | Extra virgin olive oil | 30 ml |
| 2 tbsp | Brown rice vinegar | 30 ml |
| 1 cup | Green pepper, chopped fine | 250 ml |
| 1 cup | Red pepper, chopped fine | 250 ml |
| 28 oz can | Tomato purée or crushed tomatoes | 796 ml |
| 1 1/2 cups | Textured vegetable protein (TVP) | 375 ml |
| as desired | Soy or cheddar cheese, grated | as desired |
| as desired | Sour cream or yogurt | as desired |
| | Avocado Salsa (see page 99) | |

*...continued on page 98*

# Vegetarian Black Bean Chili

*...continued from page 97*

**Method:**

Soak the beans in plenty of water for several hours or overnight.

Drain off the soaking water and simmer in fresh boiling water, partly covered, until tender (1 hour). Check the water level during cooking, adding more if necessary. Transfer the cooked beans to a large saucepan, along with 2 to 3 cups of the bean cooking water.

In a heavy skillet, sauté garlic, seasonings, rice vinegar and peppers in olive oil over medium heat until the peppers are tender. Add the pepper sauté to the cooked beans along with the tomato purée. Simmer, covered, over low heat, stirring occasionally for 20 minutes.

Add textured soy protein and continue to simmer over low heat for another 25 minutes. If necessary, add tomato juice or water to replace moisture. Serve with grated soy cheese (or cheddar cheese), sour cream or yogurt and Avocado Salsa (see page 99). *Note: If using canned beans, omit salt.* **Yields 6 - 8 servings.**

# Avocado Salsa

*This has the tomatoey spiciness of salsa and the avocadoey smoothness of guacamole. If you make only one Mexican-inspired fresh condiment, let it be our wonderful Avocado Salsa.*

Ingredients:

| | | |
|---|---|---|
| 2 | Fresh tomatoes, seeded and diced | 2 |
| 1/2 | Red onion, chopped | 1/2 |
| 1 - 2 | Jalapeño pepper, seeded and minced | 1 - 2 |
| 1/2 cup | Fresh cilantro, chopped | 125 ml |
| 2 tbsp | Extra virgin olive oil | 30 ml |
| 2 tbsp | Lime juice | 30 ml |
| 2 | Avocados | 2 |
| to taste | Sea salt | to taste |

Method:

Combine first 6 ingredients in medium bowl. Season to taste with salt. If tomatoes are not fully ripe, add a scant teaspoon of sugar. Add avocado to salsa just before serving. Can be covered and refrigerated for up to 2 days.

Bulgar Pecan Pilaf

Emerald Sesame Kale

Mashed Sweet Potatoes
with Raisins and Ginger

Carrot, Beet and
Parsnip Rosti

Quinoa Sunflower
Surprise

Savoury Red Cabbage
with Apples and Spices

Sesame Green Beans

# 10
## Sides –
## *Show Off Your*
## *Best Side*

Like the Best Supporting Actor or Actress, a good side dish needs to work hard without stealing the show. And a meal with a dull but reliable main course – like a movie with a dull but reliable lead actor – can be saved by an intriguing side dish. So whether it's the delicious surprise of our non-potato rosti, or just a beautifully simple classic couscous, explore your creative side – by making a creative side!

**PLANET
ORGANIC**
M A R K E T

# Bulgar Pecan Pilaf

*If you (or anyone you cook for) are leery of whole grains, try this excellent pilaf. This delicious side dish uses two different kinds – both brown rice and bulgar wheat are complex carbohydrates. Pecans, currants and parsley add a nice extra touch of texture and flavour.*

**Serving Tip**
This pilaf is delicious reheated – just place in ovenproof dish and bake 20-30 minutes in a 325°F oven.

### Ingredients:

| | | |
|---|---|---|
| 2 tbsp | Butter | 30 ml |
| 1/2 cup | Onion, diced | 125 ml |
| 1/2 cup | Bulgar wheat | 125 ml |
| 1/2 cup | Brown rice | 125 ml |
| 1/2 tsp | Turmeric | 2 ml |
| 1/3 cup | Currants | 80 ml |
| 1/3 cup | Pecans, chopped | 80 ml |
| 2 tbsp | Fresh parsley, chopped | 30 ml |
| 2 cups | Vegetable or chicken stock | 500 ml |
| 1 tbsp | Lemon juice | 15 ml |
| 1 tsp | Lemon zest | 5 ml |
| to taste | Sea salt | to taste |
| to taste | Freshly ground black pepper | to taste |

### Method:

In a large saucepan over medium heat, add butter and melt. When melted, add onion, bulgar, brown rice and turmeric and cook until golden, 3-5 minutes. Add currants and stock, reduce heat, cover and simmer 35-45 minutes until all liquid is absorbed. Remove from heat, add remaining ingredients, toss and serve hot. **Yields 4 - 6 servings.**

# Emerald Sesame Kale

**Kale**

Kale grows well in
northern climates and
is best in winter and early
spring. It also improves
in taste after a light frost.

*Why are we such kale pushers? Simple: it has more nutritional value per calorie than almost any other food. Although kale is quite chewy when raw, a light stir-fry will make it much more tender, improve its flavour and brighten the colour.*

## Ingredients:

| | | |
|---|---|---|
| 2 bunches | Kale, centre stems removed | 2 bunches |
| 3 tbsp | Toasted sesame oil | 45 ml |
| 1 - 2 tbsp | Tamari | 15 - 30 ml |
| 4 tsp | Garlic, minced | 20 ml |
| 3 tbsp | Sesame seeds | 45 ml |

## Method:

In a large skillet, sauté oil, garlic and tamari, being careful not to burn the garlic. Add the kale and stir-fry until soft but still bright green.

Do not overcook. Place kale in bowl and toss with sesame seeds while still hot. **Yields 4 -6 servings.**

# Mashed Sweet Potatoes with Raisins and Ginger

*Mashed potatoes appeal to everyone. This recipe uses sweet potatoes, raisins and ginger to make a slightly sweeter and spicier side dish that would be comfortable – and comforting – with almost any meal. Yogurt can easily replace the sour cream without losing any flavour.*

Ingredients:

| | | |
|---|---|---|
| 2 lbs | Sweet potatoes (yams), cubed | 1 kg |
| 1/3 cup | Sour cream or plain yogurt, full-fat | 80 ml |
| 1/4 cup | Raisins | 60 ml |
| 3 tbsp | Butter | 45 ml |
| 1/2 tsp | Ginger, ground | 2 ml |
| 1 tbsp | Brown sugar | 15 ml |
| 1/4 tsp | Sea salt | 1 ml |
| to taste | Freshly ground black pepper | to taste |

Method:

In a large pot, place cubed sweet potatoes and cover with water and bring to a boil. Reduce heat and cook 15-20 minutes or until tender. Remove from heat and drain.

In a large bowl, mix sour cream, raisins, butter, ginger, sugar, salt and pepper in pot and add in the potatoes. Mash until potatoes are smooth and all ingredients are combined. Serve hot. **Yields 6 servings.**

# Carrot, Beet and Parsnip Rosti

**Party Idea**

Instead of fondue, have a rosti party – just make sure you have plenty of sour cream for dipping!

*Rosti are traditional Swiss fried potato cakes. They're even better when made with other veggies.*

## Ingredients:

| | | |
|---|---|---|
| 3 cups | Carrots, peeled and grated | 750 ml |
| 1 cup | Beets, peeled and grated | 250 ml |
| 1 cup | Parsnips, peeled and grated | 250 ml |
| 2 | Eggs | 2 |
| 1/3 cup | Unbleached white flour | 80 ml |
| 1/2 tsp | Sea salt | 2 ml |
| 1/4 tsp | Freshly ground black pepper | 1 ml |
| 1/4 cup | Canola oil (for frying) | 60 ml |
| 1/4 cup | Sour cream or plain yogurt, full-fat | 60 ml |
| 1 tsp | Cumin, ground | 5 ml |
| 1/2 tsp | Dill, dried | 2 ml |

## Method:

Preheat oven to 350°F. In a small bowl, mix sour cream, cumin and dill. Refrigerate until needed. In a large bowl, mix together grated veggies, eggs, flour, salt and pepper until well combined. Divide mixture into twelve patties and put on a large sheet of parchment paper.

Heat a frying pan over medium heat. Add 1 tablespoon of oil to pan and let it heat up, add four patties of carrot mixture. Press patties into pancakes and fry on each side 3-5 minutes or until golden brown on both sides.

Place on a baking tray and bake 10-15 minutes. Remove from oven and serve with sour cream sauce if desired. **Yields 12 cakes.**

# Quinoa Sunflower Surprise

*Quinoa was the sacred grain of the Inca, and apparently the Incan emperor sowed the first ceremonial seeds each season using golden implements. Which is all very well, but let's not overlook the fact that this highly nutritious seed also makes a delicious side dish, too. Be sure to rinse quinoa thoroughly before cooking; it has a bitter taste if not washed and rinsed well.*

## Quinoa

Quinoa is a protein-rich seed with a fluffy, creamy, slightly crunchy texture. When cooked, it has a nutty flavour. Although it appears to be a grain, it is actually the seed of a leafy vegetable.

## Sunflower Seeds

Sunflower seeds are full of healthy fats, protein, fibre, minerals, vitamin E and phytochemicals.

Ingredients:

| | | |
|---|---|---|
| 1 cup | Quinoa, rinsed | 250 ml |
| 2 cups | Water | 500 ml |
| 1/2 cup | Carrots, grated | 125 ml |
| 1/4 cup | Green onions, thinly sliced | 60 ml |
| 1/4 cup | Fresh parsley, chopped | 60 ml |
| 1/4 cup | Sunflower seeds, toasted | 60 ml |
| 1 tbsp | Sunflower oil | 15 ml |
| 2 tbsp | Apple cider vinegar | 30 ml |
| 1 tbsp | Lemon juice | 15 ml |
| 1 tbsp | Tamari | 15 ml |
| 1 1/2 tsp | Freshly ground black pepper | 7 ml |

Method:

In a medium-sized pot bring water to a boil. Add quinoa, reduce heat to medium and cook until tender, 12-15 minutes. Drain and spread on a baking sheet to cool.

In a large bowl mix all remaining ingredients and toss with cooled quinoa until well combined. Serve chilled or warm. Salad keeps refrigerated 2-3 days. **Yields 6 servings.**

# Savoury Red Cabbage with Apples and Spices

*Cabbage and apples are a classic combination, and they both store well so they're readily available throughout the year. This recipe adds the spicy warmth of cloves and cinnamon.*

## Ingredients:

| | | |
|---|---|---|
| 10 cups | Red cabbage, shredded | 2.25 L |
| 2 | Apples, tart | 2 |
| 1 tsp | Sea salt | 5 ml |
| 1/2 - 3/4 cup | Water | 125 - 180 ml |
| 2 tsp | Granulated cane sugar | 2 ml |
| 1 - 2 tbsp | Apple cider vinegar | 15 - 30 ml |
| 2 tbsp | Butter | 30 ml |
| 1/2 tsp | Cloves, ground | 2 ml |
| 1 | Bay leaf | 1 |
| 1/8 tsp | Freshly ground black pepper | .5 ml |
| pinch | Cinnamon, ground | pinch |

## Method:

Remove hard outer leaves of cabbage. Cut into quarters, remove white inner core and with a sharp knife shred finely.

Peel, core and slice apples and place in a Dutch oven along with cabbage, bay leaf, salt and water. Don't add too much water. Watch carefully during cooking to make sure it doesn't dry out; add a little water as you go. Cook until cabbage is soft and water has been absorbed (about 45 minutes to 1 hour).

Add butter, sugar, vinegar, cinnamon and cloves. Taste and adjust the vinegar. Remove bay leaf and serve. **Yields 4 - 6 servings.**

# Sesame Green Beans

*Green beans are another nutritional star that don't always get the respect they deserve. Toasted sesame oil adds a beautiful, smoky taste to this Asian-influenced vegetable dish.*

## Ingredients:

| | | |
|---|---|---|
| 2 lbs | Green beans | 1 kg |
| 3 tbsp | Toasted sesame oil | 45 ml |
| 1 tbsp | Bragg Liquid Aminos | 15 ml |
| 1 tbsp | Black sesame seeds (optional) | 15 ml |
| 1 tsp | Chilies, dried (optional) | 5 ml |

## Method:

Bring a large pot of water to a boil and add beans (trim ends first). Cook 2-5 minutes until tender. Remove from heat and drain.

Mix oil, Bragg Liquid Aminos, sesame seeds and chilies in pot and add drained hot beans. Toss to evenly coat and serve. *Note: For the best results, cook fresh beans in at least 5 litres of boiling water. This recipe also works beautifully with broccoli, chard, bok choy or kale – all very healthy alternatives.* **Yields 4 - 6 servings.**

---

**Green Beans**

Green beans are an excellent source of vitamins A, C and K, manganese, dietary fiber, potassium, folate and iron, and a good source of magnesium, thiamine, riboflavin, copper, calcium, phosphorus, protein, omega-3 fatty acids and niacin. There's a reason your mother told you to "finish your beans!"

# 11

# Breakfast –
## *Smart Starts*

Breakfast deserves more respect. If we're pressed for time, it's the first to go. Yet study after study proves that your mother was right: it is the most important meal of the day. For weight loss, lower cholesterol, better memory and much more, a healthy breakfast helps you all day, every day. Our breakfast recipes are a great start – they're full of healthy carbs, such as fruit and whole grains, and healthy proteins. The only thing better than a healthy breakfast? Getting to sleep in and have a healthy brunch instead!

PLANET
ORGANIC
M A R K E T

# Blueberry Pineapple Bran Muffins

## Ingredients:

| | | |
|---|---|---|
| 1/2 cup | Canola oil | 125 ml |
| 1/3 cup | Blackstrap molasses | 80 ml |
| 1/3 cup | Pure honey | 80 ml |
| 1 | Egg | 1 |
| 1/2 tsp | Pure vanilla extract | 2 ml |
| 2 cups | Bran flakes | 500 ml |
| 1/4 cup | Pineapple, crushed | 60 ml |
| 1 cup | Buttermilk | 250 ml |
| 3/4 cup | Unbleached white flour | 180 ml |
| 1/3 cup | Whole wheat flour | 80 ml |
| 1 1/2 tsp | Baking powder | 7 ml |
| 1 1/2 tsp | Baking soda | 7 ml |
| 1/2 tsp | Sea salt | 2 ml |
| 1 cup | Blueberries | 250 ml |

## Method:

Preheat oven to 350°F. In a mixer combine oil, molasses, honey, egg and vanilla for one minute. Add bran flakes, pineapple and buttermilk and mix for an additional minute.

Add dry ingredients except blueberries and mix on low speed until batter is smooth and well combined. Stir blueberries in by hand (do not over-mix and bleed berries). Scoop into 12 lined or greased muffin cups and bake 30 minutes or until done. Remove from oven and serve warm. **Yields 12 muffins.**

*Ready to build a better bran muffin? Buttermilk, pineapple and two kinds of natural sweeteners make these muffins tender, healthy and oh so good for you.*

### Blueberries

Blueberries are nutritional superstars – full of flavour, yet low in calories. Current studies show that blueberries have antioxidant capabilities, which can help destroy free radicals! Blueberries are also a great source of vitamin C, vitamin E and fibre.

### Cooking Tip

Batter will keep 3-4 days refrigerated until baked.

# Ginger Scones

## Cooking Tip

In a food processor, mix the crystallized ginger with 1 cup of flour and pulse until ginger is finely chopped. This extra step ensures evenly chopped ginger.

## Half Recipe

Want to make only 6 scones? The dry mix keeps well in a zip-lock bag. Just add 3 cups of dry with 1 1/2 cups buttermilk and 6 tablespoons canola oil. Follow the regular mixing/baking instructions.

*Sometimes breakfast needs a little zing. The candied ginger turns these reliable buttermilk scones into scones with zing. Enjoy!*

## Ingredients:

| | | |
|---|---|---|
| 5 cups | Unbleached white flour | 1.10 kg |
| 1/2 cup | Granulated cane sugar | 125 ml |
| 1 tsp | Baking soda | 5 ml |
| 1 3/4 tsp | Sea salt | 8 ml |
| 1/2 cup | Crystallized ginger, finely chopped | 125 ml |
| 3 cups | Buttermilk | 750 ml |
| 3/4 cup | Canola oil | 180 ml |

## Method:

Preheat oven to 350°F degrees. Prepare baking trays with parchment paper.

In a large bowl, mix dry ingredients together: flour, sugar, baking soda, salt and ginger. In a medium bowl, blend the buttermilk and oil. Add the wet mixture to the dry until moist (do not over-mix).

Use a large ice cream scoop to form scones. Place on parchment lined tray and press down with palm of your hand to flatten. Bake until golden (about 25 minutes). **Yields 12 scones.**

# Gluten-free Light-as-a-Feather Muffins

*What if a muffin could fly? Well, they can't. But these muffins come deliciously close — our recipe testers said they were a "miracle." So make a miracle happen in your kitchen and make these for your guests or friends who can't eat gluten.*

**Variation**

Add 1/2 cup raisins, 1/2 cup walnut pieces and 1 cup diced apples.

Ingredients:

| | | |
|---|---|---|
| 3 cups | Featherlight Flour Mix (see page 115) | 750 ml |
| 2 tsp | Xanthan gum | 10 ml |
| 1 1/2 tsp | Baking soda | 7 ml |
| 1 tsp | Sea salt | 5 ml |
| 1 tsp | Nutmeg, ground | 5 ml |
| 1 tbsp | Cinnamon, ground | 15 ml |
| 3/4 cup | Almond, rice, goat or soy milk | 180 ml |
| 3/4 cup | Pure maple syrup (or fruit sweetened jam) | 180 ml |
| 2/3 cup | Butter, melted and cooled | 160 ml |
| 1/3 cup | Blackstrap molasses | 80 ml |
| 1 1/2 tsp | Pure vanilla extract | 7 ml |
| 2 | Eggs, well beaten | 2 |

Method:

Preheat oven to 375°F. Mix dry ingredients. Mix wet ingredients.

In a large bowl, combine wet and dry ingredients until well blended. Let batter sit for 5 minutes as it will slightly thicken. Fill prepared muffin tins 3/4 full and bake in 375°F oven for 35 minutes. After the first 10 minutes, cover with foil to avoid over darkening. Do not underbake. **Yields 6 large muffins.**

# Gluten-free Featherlight Flour Mix

### Sorghum Flour

A gluten-free diet is followed by people who have celiac disease or are gluten sensitive, or choose to follow a gluten-free diet. This mixture of sorghum, tapioca and arrowroot flour is an excellent substitute for those who cannot tolerate gluten.

### Cooking Tip

This is a terrific gluten-free base which can be used in baking muffins and breads.

## Ingredients:

| | | |
|---|---|---|
| 4 cups | Sorghum flour | 1 L |
| 4 cups | Tapioca flour | 1 L |
| 4 1/4 cups | Arrowroot flour | 1.06 L |

## Method:

Use your hands to incorporate the different flours. Store and use as needed. **Yields 12 cups.**

# Mocha Muffins

*What if you could get everything that belongs in a breakfast – orange juice, yogurt, eggs, coffee – into a muffin? Wouldn't that be great? What if you could do all that, plus chocolate? That would be better than great.*

Ingredients:

| | | |
|---|---|---|
| 1/2 cup | Butter, softened | 125 ml |
| 1 1/3 cups | Granulated cane sugar | 330 ml |
| 1/2 cup | Canola oil | 125 ml |
| 2 | Eggs | 2 |
| 2/3 cup | Plain yogurt, full-fat | 160 ml |
| 1/4 cup | Orange juice | 60 ml |
| 2 tbsp | Brewed coffee | 30 ml |
| 3 cups | Unbleached white flour | 750 ml |
| 1 tsp | Baking powder | 5 ml |
| 1/2 tsp | Baking soda | 2 ml |
| 2 tbsp | Fresh coffee beans, ground* | 30 ml |
| 1 cup | Dark chocolate (chunks or chips) | 250 ml |

## Method:

Preheat oven to 350°F. Prepare muffin tins.

In a large bowl mix together the flour, baking powder, baking soda, ground coffee and set aside. Mix the oil, butter, eggs and sugar in separate bowl for 2 minutes. Add the brewed coffee, orange juice and yogurt. Stir this mixture into the dry ingredients just until flour is moistened.

Fold in dark chocolate (chunks or chips). Divide batter evenly into 12 large or 18 regular muffin cups. Bake 20-30 minutes or until toothpick inserted into centre comes out clean. **Yields 12 - 18 muffins.**

*Yes, we mean actual coffee grounds are added to the mix. They add the wonderful coffee flecks and flavour.

# O Canada Waffles

*Maple syrup and waffles belong together, so we started by adding it to the batter. Impress your weekend guests with this patriotically Canadian version of waffles. Cornmeal adds texture, and yogurt makes them tender.*

Ingredients:

| | | |
|---|---|---|
| 1 cup | Unbleached white flour | 250 ml |
| 1 cup | Yellow cornmeal, fine | 250 ml |
| 1 1/2 tsp | Baking powder | 7 ml |
| 3/4 tsp | Sea salt | 4 ml |
| 1/2 tsp | Baking soda | 2 ml |
| 1 cup | Plain yogurt, full-fat | 250 ml |
| 1/2 cup | Water | 125 ml |
| 1/4 cup | Pure maple syrup | 60 ml |
| 2 tbsp | Canola oil | 30 ml |
| 1 | Egg yolk | 1 |
| 2 | Egg whites | 2 |

Method:
Preheat waffle iron.

In a large bowl combine flour, cornmeal, baking powder, salt and baking soda. Set aside. In another bowl, stir together yogurt, water, maple syrup, oil and egg yolk. Set aside. Beat egg whites until stiff peaks form. Set aside.

Combine the dry ingredients with the wet. Fold in the egg whites. For each waffle, scoop 1/4 - 1/2 cup of batter onto iron. Close the lid and bake according to waffle iron instructions and size. Serve hot. Pop in the toaster to reheat cold waffles. **Yields 6 - 8 servings.**

# Organic Granola

*The mixture of oats, almonds, cashews and dried berries is a great snack for those busy mornings and after-school snacks. Oats are a wonderful source of soluble fibre, which is known to help reduce high blood cholesterol. Almonds are a crunchy favourite that are convenient as well as nutritious. Some studies show that a handful of almonds a day can help lower LDL cholesterol.*

Ingredients:

| | | |
|---|---|---|
| 3 cups | Slow-cooking oat flakes | 750 ml |
| 1 cup | Almonds, slivered | 250 ml |
| 1 cup | Cashew pieces | 250 ml |
| 3/4 cup | Coconut flakes, unsweetened | 180 ml |
| 1/4 cup | Brown sugar | 60 ml |
| 1/2 tsp | Sea salt | 2 ml |
| 1/3 cup | Pure maple syrup | 80 ml |
| 1/4 cup | Canola oil | 60 ml |
| 1 cup | Dried cranberries or blueberries | 250 ml |
| 1 cup | Raisins | 250 ml |

Method:

Preheat oven to 250°F. In a large bowl combine oats, almonds, cashews, coconut, sugar and salt. Set aside. Whisk together maple syrup and oil and pour over oat mix. Divide mixture onto two baking trays and place in oven.

Bake 1-2 hours, stirring every 20 minutes to achieve an even browning. When desired color is achieved, remove from oven and cool. Place in a large bowl and toss with desired berries and raisins. Store in an airtight container. **Yields 6 cups.**

# Tofu Scramble

*Whether you want to eat fewer eggs or more tofu, this recipe is the answer. Similar to scrambled eggs, this is a nice spicy way to start your day.*

## Ingredients:

| | | |
|---|---|---|
| 1 lb | Tofu, firm | 500 g |
| 1 tbsp | Canola oil | 15 ml |
| 1/2 cup | Onion, diced | 125 ml |
| 1/2 cup | Celery, diced | 125 ml |
| 1/2 cup | Red or green pepper, diced | 125 ml |
| 1 tbsp | Tamari | 15 ml |
| 1 tsp | Basil, dried | 5 ml |
| 1/2 tsp | Curry powder | 2 ml |
| 1/2 tsp | Garlic powder | 2 ml |
| to taste | Freshly ground black pepper | to taste |
| | Turmeric (optional) | |

## Method:

Drain tofu and mash until crumbly, set aside in a medium-sized bowl.

In a large pan, heat oil and add diced vegetables. Cook over medium heat 2-3 minutes. Add tofu, tamari and spices. Cook for 5-10 minutes, stirring frequently. Remove from heat and serve immediately. **Yields 4 servings.**

# Wild Smoked Salmon Frittata

*If you love smoked salmon with cream cheese and onions on a bagel, then this is your kind of frittata. Add a nice toasted multigrain bagel on the side? Why not!*

Ingredients:

| | | |
|---|---|---|
| 8 | Eggs | 8 |
| 2/3 cup | Whole milk | 160 ml |
| 2 tbsp | Chives, finely chopped | 30 ml |
| 1 tsp | Freshly ground black pepper | 5 ml |
| 2 tbsp | Butter | 30 ml |
| 1 cup | Red onion, thinly sliced | 250 ml |
| 1/4 cup | Cream cheese, cubed | 60 ml |
| 1/2 cup | Wild smoked salmon, chopped | 125 ml |
| 2 - 3 | Fresh tomatoes, sliced | 2 - 3 |

Method:

Preheat oven to 375°F. In a bowl whisk eggs until frothy. Add milk, chives and pepper and set aside. In a large ovenproof skillet, heat butter until melted.

With heat at medium, add egg mixture to pan and then quickly arrange onions, cheese, salmon and tomatoes on top evenly. Cook for 3 minutes on stove-top without stirring, then transfer to oven. Bake until the top is golden brown and let set, about 20-30 minutes, or until centre is set. Remove from oven and cool slightly before serving. **Yields 6 - 8 servings**.

# Golden Tropical Compote

**Fruit Enzymes**

Papaya, mango and pineapple all contain healthy enzymes and have been used for centuries to aid digestion. It's a healthy and delicious way to end a meal.

*Fruit compote is one of those things it's nice to find in the fridge. With so many wonderful unsulphured dried tropical fruits now available, it's fun to try a completely different flavour experience.*

### Ingredients:

| | | |
|---|---|---|
| 1 1/2 lbs | Dried fruit (papaya, mango, apples, pineapple, apricots) | 750 g |
| 1/4 cup | Crystallized ginger, chopped | 60 ml |
| 1 cup | Orange juice | 250 ml |
| 1/4 cup | Lemon juice | 60 ml |
| 1/3 cup | Pure maple syrup | 80 ml |
| 1 cup | Water | 250 ml |

### Method:

Cut large pieces of fruit into smaller sizes. In a medium-sized saucepan, put in fruit and cover with lemon juice, orange juice, maple syrup and water. Soak for 30 minutes.

Cook the fruit at a low simmer for about 15 minutes or until just tender, adding more water if it gets too thick. Serve the compote either warm or cold. Excellent as a dessert over ice cream or for breakfast with yogurt and granola. Keeps for a long time in the refrigerator. **Yields 4 - 6 servings.**

Chai Pound Cake
with Apricot Glaze

Cherry Berry Compote

Chocolate Quinoa Cake

Fresh Apple/Pear
Everyday Cake

Old-fashioned
Rice Pudding

Almond Apple Crumble

Organic Bean Brownie
with Chocolate Tofu Icing

Trans Fat-free Pie Crust

Organic Fruit Pie Filling

PLANET
ORGANIC
M A R K E T

# 12
# Desserts –
## *Guilt-free Goodness*

Some people believe that eating healthy includes skipping dessert. We don't believe dessert is bad for you. We believe bad food is bad for you. When you make a dessert with healthy, natural ingredients such as organic butter, organic fruits, granulated cane sugar and organic fair trade chocolate, it can be uniquely satisfying and nourishing. Of course, moderation is always healthy – but so is taking pleasure in your food. And for us, that often includes the pleasure of dessert.

# Chai Pound Cake with Apricot Glaze

*Nothing goes better with pound cake than a nice cup of tea. This pound cake recipe uses cloves, cardamom, fennel and cinnamon to add the soothing warmth and spiciness of chai tea to the cake.*

## Ingredients:

| | | |
|---|---|---|
| 2 1/4 cups | Unbleached white flour | 560 ml |
| 1 1/2 tsp | Baking powder | 7 ml |
| 1/2 tsp | Sea salt | 2 ml |
| 2 tsp | Cinnamon, ground | 10 ml |
| 1 tsp | Allspice, ground | 5 ml |
| 1/2 tsp | Ginger, ground | 2 ml |
| 1/2 tsp | Cardamom, ground | 2 ml |
| 1 cup | Butter, softened | 250 ml |
| 1/2 cup | Cream cheese, softened | 125 ml |
| 1 cup | Granulated cane sugar | 250 ml |
| 4 | Eggs | 4 |
| 2 tsp | Pure vanilla extract | 10 ml |

## Chai Spice:

| | | |
|---|---|---|
| 1/2 tsp | Cloves, ground | 2 ml |
| 1 tsp | Cardamom, ground | 5 ml |
| 1 tsp | Fennel, ground | 5 ml |
| 1/2 tsp | Cinnamon, ground | 2 ml |

## Glaze:

| 2 tbsp | Apricot jam | 30 ml |
| 2 tbsp | Lemon juice | 30 ml |
| 1 tbsp | Chai spice | 15 ml |

## Method:

Preheat oven to 350°F. Grease and flour a 10" bundt pan.

Sift together flour, powder, salt and spices. Set aside.

In a mixer, cream butter, cream cheese, sugar, eggs and vanilla. Slowly add the flour mixture until all is well combined.

Pour batter into pan and bake for 60-75 minutes or until a toothpick inserted comes out clean. Remove from oven and let cool for 10 minutes.

Glaze: gently heat the jam and juice. Pass through sieve. In a bowl whisk together chai spice and glaze mixture to make a glaze. Invert cake onto a platter and top with glaze slowly to allow glaze to soak in and not run off the cake. *Note: You can omit the glaze and serve with natural ice cream.* **Yields one 10" bundt cake.**

# Cherry Berry Compote

*Fruit compotes are popular around the world – they're easy to make, healthy, soothing and delicious. During the winter months, compotes are great as breakfast foods or heated and served over ice cream for a splendid dessert.*

## Ingredients:

| 1 1/2 lbs | Dried fruit: cranberries, blueberries, raisins, prunes (halved), black mission figs, Turkish apricots, cherries, etc. | 750 g |
|-----------|---------------------------------------------------------------------------------------------------------------------|-------|
| 2 cups | Apple cider or juice | 500 ml |
| 1 cup | Water | 250 ml |
| 1 | Cinnamon stick (optional) | 1 |
| 1/2 tbsp | Lemon zest (optional) | 7 ml |

## Method:

Place fruit in a large pan and cover with apple cider and water. Soak for 30 minutes. Cook the fruit and simmer over low heat in the same water for about 15 minutes or until just tender, adding more water if it gets too thick.

Serve the compote either warm or cold. If you like a sweeter version, add some sugar while simmering.

*Note: Compotes are excellent for dessert when served over ice cream, or for breakfast with yogurt and granola. Compotes will keep for a long time in the refrigerator.* **Yields 4 - 6 servings.**

### Dried Fruit

Cranberries – high in vitamin C.

Blueberries – antioxidant superstars.

Raisins – high in iron and minerals, raisins are the most popular of all the dried fruits.

Prunes – rich in iron.

Turkish apricots – rich in iron, phosphorous, calcium and vitamin A.

Cherries – high in vitamins A and B1, iron, copper and manganese.

Figs – high in iron, calcium, phosphorous, B vitamins and folic acid.

# Chocolate Quinoa Cake

*This healthy cake brings together the chocolate of the Mayan empire with the protein-rich Quinoa of the Aztecs to create a rich, yet delicate treat.*

**Honey**

Honey, the champion of the natural food world, is rich in enzymes, contains some minerals and usually contains some B vitamins and vitamin C.

## Ingredients:

| | | |
|---|---|---|
| 1 cup | Quinoa, rinsed | 250 ml |
| 2 cups | Apple cider or juice | 500 ml |
| 3/4 cup | Butter | 180 ml |
| 2/3 cup | Fair trade cocoa powder | 160 ml |
| 3/4 cup | Pure honey | 180 ml |
| 3/4 cup | Brown rice syrup | 180 ml |
| 1 tsp | Pure vanilla extract | 5 ml |
| 1 1/2 cups | Milk or soy milk | 375 ml |
| 3 | Eggs | 3 |
| 2 cups | Quinoa flour | 500 ml |
| 1 cup | Unbleached white flour | 250 ml |
| 1 tsp | Baking powder | 5 ml |
| 1 tsp | Sea salt | 5 ml |
| 1/3 cup | Hazelnuts, toasted and ground fine | 80 ml |

## Method:

Preheat oven to 325°F. Prepare quinoa by rinsing under water for one minute. Drain. In a medium-sized sauce pan, bring the apple juice to a boil and add quinoa. Reduce heat to a simmer and cook, covered for 20 minutes or until all juice is absorbed. Remove from heat, fluff with a fork and set aside.

In a mixer, cream butter, cocoa, rice syrup, honey and vanilla. Add eggs and mix until combined. Combine flours, baking powder, salt and nuts and add alternately with milk, stirring by hand until well combined. Fold in cooled quinoa and spread batter into a greased or lined baking pan.

Bake 35 minutes or until toothpick inserted comes out clean. Remove from oven and cool completely before icing. Use the Chocolate Glaze recipe on page 21 for an added touch of flavour. **Yields 10 servings.**

# Fresh Apple/Pear Everyday Cake

## Ingredients:

| | | |
|---|---|---|
| 1/3 cup | Butter | 80 ml |
| 1 cup | Granulated cane sugar | 250 ml |
| 2 | Eggs | 2 |
| 1 tsp | Pure vanilla extract | 5 ml |
| 1 1/2 cups | Whole wheat pastry flour | 375 ml |
| 1 tsp | Baking powder | 5 ml |
| 1 tsp | Baking soda | 5 ml |
| 1/2 tsp | Sea salt | 2 ml |
| 1/2 tsp | Cinnamon, ground | 2 ml |
| 1/2 tsp | Nutmeg, ground | 2 ml |
| 1/2 tsp | Allspice, ground | 2 ml |
| 1/8 tsp | Cloves, ground | .5 ml |
| 2 cups | Apples or pears, finely chopped | 500 ml |
| 1/2 cup | Raisins (optional) | 125 ml |
| 1/2 cup | Walnuts (optional) | 125 ml |

*How often to you need a delicious cake that's easy to make and doesn't take long? Just like the name says – every day! You can make a cream cheese frosting, but it's just as good plain.*

**Apples**

Apples are always fall and winter fruit basics – high in magnesium, iron, potassium and pectin, they even aid in digestion. Organic farming has helped bring back a number of heritage apples with a variety of flavours, sweetness and crispness. Try Braeburn, Gala, Honeycomb, or Jonagold.

## Method:

Preheat the oven to 350°F. Grease and flour an 8" round or square pan.

In a large mixing bowl or food processor, beat the butter until it is smooth. Add the sugar and continue to beat until well blended. Add the eggs and vanilla and beat well. Combine flour, baking powder, baking soda, salt, spices and sift together into the butter-sugar mix. Beat until smooth; the mixture will be very stiff.

Add the apple, raisins and nuts (if using) and beat well. Spread evenly in the pan. Bake for 35 - 40 minutes, or until a toothpick inserted in the centre comes out clean. Remove from the oven and cool on a rack. Serve warm or cooled. **Yields 8 servings.**

# Old-fashioned Rice Pudding

## Brown Rice

Short grain brown rice has a full flavour. After cooking, the grains become soft and cling together. For this reason, short grain brown rice is well suited to recipes where a creamy texture is needed, such as puddings.

## Cooking Tip

Substitute your favourite dried fruit for raisins.

*This nursery food becomes a terrific healthy dessert or breakfast when made with whole grain brown rice and honey or maple syrup. Make sure to use whole milk — the extra fat is needed to make the pudding creamy.*

### Ingredients:

| | | |
|---|---|---|
| 2 cups | Basmati or brown rice, cooked | 500 ml |
| 2 cups | Milk, soy, rice or cow (not skim) | 500 ml |
| 1/2 tsp | Sea salt | 2 ml |
| 1/4 cup | Pure honey or maple syrup | 60 ml |
| 1 tsp | Pure vanilla extract | 5 ml |
| 1/2 tsp | Cinnamon, ground | 2 ml |
| 1/4 tsp | Nutmeg, ground | 1 ml |
| 1/2 cup | Raisins | 125 ml |
| 2 tsp | Lemon juice | 10 ml |

### Method:

In a heavy-bottomed saucepan, place cooked rice and milk and cook over high heat until it comes to a boil. Reduce heat and simmer covered for 20-25 minutes or until milk is mostly absorbed.

Remove from heat and add remaining ingredients until well combined.

Serve warm or cooled. **Yields 4 servings**.

# Almond Apple Crumble

*Almonds add protein and other important nutrients to this tasty, homey dessert.*

Ingredients:

| | | |
|---|---|---|
| 1 cup | Butter, softened | 250 ml |
| 3/4 cup | Brown sugar | 180 ml |
| 1/2 cup | Unbleached white flour | 125 ml |
| 4 cups | Slow-cooking oat flakes | 1 L |
| 1/2 cup | Almonds, slivered (optional) | 125 ml |
| 6 cups | Apples, peeled, cored and chopped | 1.5 L |
| 1 cup | Brown sugar | 250 ml |
| 2 tbsp | Unbleached white flour | 30 ml |
| 1 tsp | Cinnamon, ground | 5 ml |
| dash | Nutmeg, ground | dash |
| pinch | Sea salt | pinch |
| 2 tbsp | Lemon juice | 30 ml |
| 2 tbsp | Butter | 30 ml |

Cinnamon-scented whipped cream:

| | | |
|---|---|---|
| 1 cup | Heavy cream | 250 ml |
| 1/4 cup | Granulated cane sugar | 60 ml |
| 1/2 tsp | Cinnamon, ground | 2 ml |
| 1 tsp | Pure vanilla extract | 5 ml |

## Almonds

No wonder almonds are becoming nutritional superstars – high in potassium, magnesium and phosphorous, one-fifth of their weight is made of protein.

Almonds are low in saturated fat and contain many other protective nutrients – calcium and magnesium – for strong bones, vitamin E and compounds called phytochemicals, which may help protect against cardiovascular disease and even cancer.

### Method:

Preheat oven to 350°F. Prepare a 9" square pan.

In a mixer, combine first amount of butter (1 cup), sugar, flour, oats and almonds. Mix on low-medium speed until mixture is well combined and crumbly. Set aside.

In a large bowl, combine apples, brown sugar, flour, cinnamon, nutmeg, salt and lemon juice. Let sit 10 minutes until juices start to run. Place fruit mixture in pan and dot with second amount of butter (2 tablespoons) on top. Sprinkle crumble top evenly over fruit mixture and press lightly.

Place in oven and bake 25-35 minutes until golden brown and filling is bubbling around edges.

Remove from oven and let cool slightly before serving. Serve with cinnamon-scented whipped cream or your favorite vanilla ice cream.

To make cinnamon-scented whipped cream, place cream, sugar, cinnamon and vanilla in a mixer and beat on medium-high speed until medium peaks form. **Yields 8 servings**.

# Organic Bean Brownie

*Who knew you could do this with adzuki beans?*

*This unique, sweet, decadent bean brownie is tasty and a great source of protein. This one-of-a-kind recipe came from our Halifax store, and it combines the sweet flavour of cocoa powder and tofu chocolate icing with the added protein of adzuki beans.*

Ingredients:

| | | |
|---|---|---|
| 1/3 cup | Adzuki beans, dry | 80 ml |
| 1 cup | Demerara sugar | 250 ml |
| 1/3 cup | Unbleached white flour | 80 ml |
| 1/3 cup | Canola oil | 80 ml |
| 3 | Eggs | 3 |
| 1/3 cup | Fair trade cocoa powder | 80 ml |
| 1 tsp | Pure vanilla extract | 5 ml |
| 3/4 tsp | Sea salt | 3 ml |
| | **Chocolate Tofu Icing** (see page 133) | |

Method:

Preheat oven to 325°F. Grease or line a 13" x 9" pan.

Place beans in a pot, cover with lots of water and bring to a boil. Reduce heat and cook until beans are soft. Drain and rinse with cold water. Set aside.

In a food processor or blender, combine cooked beans with oil, sugar, cocoa and vanilla until smooth.

Place flour and salt in a bowl and add processed bean mixture, stirring until just combined. Whisk eggs in a separate bowl and gently add to batter.

Pour into pan and bake 20-30 minutes until set. Remove from oven and cool completely before icing. Cut into large squares. **Yields one 13" x 9" pan.**

# Chocolate Tofu Icing

## Tofu

Tofu is a soybean curd that is high in protein and is rich in iron, calcium and B vitamins. Adzuki beans are a small, deep red bean that are somewhat sweet and have a delicate texture; they are an excellent source of fibre, folate and iron.

### Ingredients:

| | | |
|---|---|---|
| 5.25 oz | Silken tofu, soft | 150 g |
| 1/3 cup | Granulated cane sugar | 80 ml |
| 1/3 cup | Fair trade cocoa powder | 80 ml |
| 2 tbsp | Tapioca flour | 30 ml |
| 1 tsp | Canola oil | 5 ml |

### Method:

Blend all ingredients in a food processor or blender until smooth. Spread over top of cooled bean brownies.

# We think of it as the *Planet Wide Web.*

For more healthy Planet Organic recipes, nutrition and health information, and to subscribe to our monthly e-newsletter Goodness, please visit our website:

## *www.planetorganic.ca*

# Trans Fat-free Pie Crust

*For those of us who grew up on solid vegetable shortening, all the bad news about trans fats is quite depressing. That's why we like to cheer ourselves up with a healthy, better pie crust! Organic butter makes a delicious, crusty pie crust. There are also several trans fat-free shortenings available. And don't be intimated by making your own crust – it's as easy as playdough!*

### Cooking Tip
Dough can also be frozen and thawed for future use.

## Ingredients:

| | | |
|---|---|---|
| 2 1/2 cups | Unbleached white flour | 625 ml |
| 1/4 tsp | Sea salt | 1 ml |
| 1 cup | Butter or trans fat-free shortening | 250 ml |
| 1/3 cup | Cold water or orange juice | 80 ml |

## Method:

In a mixer, food processor or with a pastry blender, work butter into flour and salt until butter is incorporated.

Add the water or juice and continue to mix until dough forms into a ball. Let dough rest or refrigerate for 10-20 minutes.

When ready to use, divide dough in half and roll onto a lightly floured surface to an inch bigger than your pie plate. Place dough in plate and crimp edges for a decorative crust. For traditional pie, roll second half of dough and place on top of filled pie shell and crimp edges together. With a sharp knife, cut slits in top of pastry before baking. **Yields enough dough for 2 single or 1 double 9" pies.**

# Organic Fruit Pie Filling

(see recipe on page 134)

## Variations:

**Apple**
Add 1 tsp cinnamon and a dash of nutmeg.

**Blueberry/ Blackberry**
Add a dash of cinnamon and 1 tsp lemon zest.

**Raspberry/ Strawberry Rhubarb**
Add 2 tbsp of additional flour and 1 tsp orange zest.

*Once you make your first pie, you realize it's as easy as...making a batch of muffins. Try making an organic apple pie with crisp Granny Smith apples.*

## Ingredients:

| | | |
|---|---|---|
| 4 cups | Organic fresh or frozen fruit, thawed | 1 kg |
| 1 cup | Granulated cane sugar | 250 ml |
| 1/4 cup | Unbleached white flour | 40 ml |
| dash | Sea salt | dash |

## Method:

Preheat oven to 325-350°F. Combine all ingredients together and let sit for 15-20 minutes until juices start to run. Place filling in bottom of pie shell (see recipe on page 134) and top with top crust. Crimp edges together, brush with egg wash, cut slits into pastry and place on a baking tray.

Bake approximately 40-55 minutes until golden brown and filling is bubbling. Remove from oven and cool slightly before serving.
**Yields enough filling for one 9" pie.**

ABC Juice

Fair Trade
Hot Cocoa Mix

Ginger-spiked
Orange Juice

Indian Spice Tea

Not-So-Guilty
Mocha Indulgence

Soylicious Strawberry
Smoothie

Spiced Organic
Apple Cheer

Sunny Summer
Lemonade

PLANET
ORGANIC
M A R K E T

# 13

## Beverages –
## *How 'bout a Drink?*

In a world of giant soft-drink servings and $5 coffee, our society has a bit of a drinking problem. Whether it's too many calories or not enough nutrients, we can all do a lot better by serving ourselves and our families homemade, fresh and healthy beverages. Hot or cold, sweet or spicy – let's drop the pop and get something fun and healthy into our glasses and mugs!

# ABC Juice

*This delicious juice is as easy as ABC – Apples, Beets and Carrots. Singing the ABCs with your children while you make this could be fun!*

## Ingredients:

| 4 | Apples, cored | 4 |
|---|---|---|
| 1 | Beet | 1 |
| 2 lbs | Carrots | 1 kg |

## Method:
Place apples, beet and carrots through juicer. Stir and serve immediately.
**Yields 2 - 4 servings.**

## Variation
For an added boost, add one tablespoon of your favourite greens supplement. When juicing at home, it's important to choose organically grown fruits and vegetables.

# Fair Trade Hot Cocoa Mix

## What is Fair Trade?

Fair trade is an organized social movement promoting standards for international labour, commerce and environmentalism by encouraging trade between developed and under-developed nations. Readily available fair trade goods include coffee and chocolate.

## Variation
**Spiced Mix**
Add to 1 recipe of hot cocoa mix, 1 tsp each of ground cardamom, ground cinnamon and ground ginger.

*When you choose fair trade products, you are supporting co-operative groups of farmers in developing countries. In exchange for ensuring their products meet quality standards, fair trade programs ensure that farmers are offered good working conditions and equitable wages.*

## Ingredients:

| | | |
|---|---|---|
| 1 cup | Dry powdered milk | 250 ml |
| 1/3 cup | Fair trade cocoa powder | 80 ml |
| 3/4 cup | Granulated cane sugar | 180 ml |
| pinch | Sea salt | pinch |
| 4 cups | Boiling water | 1 L |

## Method:
Combine milk powder, cocoa, sugar and salt together (no lumps!) and store in a covered container. To make cocoa, stir 1/4 cup of mix into 1 cup of boiling water. **Yields 4 servings.**

# Ginger-spiked Orange Juice

*Supplement the health benefits of your morning orange juice with the added zing of fresh ginger. Great for giving your metabolism a morning jump-start!*

### Ingredients:

| 4 cups | Orange juice, fresh squeezed | 1 L |
|--------|------------------------------|------|
| 2 tsp | Fresh ginger, finely grated | 10 ml |

### Method:
Combine juice and ginger. Serve immediately. **Yields 2 - 4 servings.**

## Ginger

Evidence suggests that ginger has natural anti-inflammatory properties. To reap the best health benefits from ginger, try to incorporate it into your diet every day. Flavour your stir-fry vegetables or Asian-inspired sauces with a half-teaspoon of sliced ginger, or enjoy a glass of ginger tea as you relax in the evening.

# Indian Spice Tea

*Aromatic, spicy and intoxicating, chai tea is an excellent alternative for the non-coffee drinker. Make yours a latte by adding steamed organic soy milk.*

Ingredients:

| | | |
|---|---|---|
| 6 cups | Water | 1.5 L |
| 1/4 cup | Fresh ginger, sliced | 60 ml |
| 1 | Orange, cut into zest strips | 1 |
| 6 | Whole cloves | 6 |
| 1/4 tsp | Fennel seeds | 1 ml |
| 2 cups | Whole milk or soy milk | 500 ml |
| 2 tbsp | Jasmine or Darjeeling tea leaves | 30 ml |
| 1/4 cup | Granulated cane sugar | 50 ml |

## Method:

In a medium-sized saucepan over low heat, combine water, ginger, orange zest, cloves and fennel seeds. Bring to a simmer and cook over low heat for 10 minutes. Add the milk and tea leaves and increase heat to medium. Cook 5 minutes and remove from heat. Steep 5 minutes. Add sugar, stir to dissolve and serve. **Yields 6 - 8 servings.**

# Not-So-Guilty Mocha Indulgence

*Reward yourself with a hot, steamy mocha. Make it with organic fair trade coffee and chocolate and the calories don't count! Trust us, we checked.*

## Ingredients:

| | | |
|---|---|---|
| 1 cup | Hot Cocoa Mix (see page 139) | 250 ml |
| 4 cups | Coffee, brewed | 1 L |
| | Whipped cream (optional) | |

## Method:

Add hot chocolate dry mix to brewed coffee. Stir to dissolve and add a dollop of whipped cream. **Yields 4 servings.**

### Cocoa

It has long been honoured for its stress-relieving (and possibly aphrodisiac) qualities, but underneath cocoa's wholesome image is a dangerous secret. It's one of the most pesticide-laden crops in the world. Years of using dangerous chemical pesticides to control their cocoa production, including the deadly Organochloride Lindane, has put the health of farmers, wildlife and consumers at risk. Recently banned in Canada and Europe, the chemical is still in use in the US and many developing countries. Could it be in your grocery-bought chocolate bar?

# Soylicious Strawberry Smoothie

**Strawberries**

Strawberries are packed with phenols, a powerful phytonutrient that helps protect cell structures and prevent oxygen damage. Make it a regular staple of your diet, especially during cold and flu season!

*Make this sweet treat using organic strawberries and fair trade organic bananas. A tasty and quick way to get fruit and protein, any time of day.*

### Ingredients:

| | | |
|---|---|---|
| 10.5 oz | Silken tofu, soft | 300 g |
| 1 cup | Papaya nectar (or other tropical juice) | 250 ml |
| 1 cup | Strawberries, fresh or frozen | 250 ml |
| 1 | Banana | 1 |
| 1 tbsp | Pure honey | 15 ml |
| 8 | Ice cubes | 8 |

### Method:

Place all ingredients in a blender and process until smooth (approximately 1-2 minutes). Serve immediately. **Yields 2 servings.**

# Spiced Organic Apple Cheer

*A glass of fresh apple cider gives you all the benefits of a whole apple – in a glass. Coupled with the detoxifying effects of citrus, it's also a healthy way to warm up on a cold day. Drink up!*

### Ingredients:

| | | |
|---|---|---|
| 4 cups | Apple cider or juice | 1 L |
| 1 cup | Pineapple juice | 250 ml |
| 1/2 cup | Orange juice | 125 ml |
| 1 tbsp | Lemon juice | 15 ml |
| 1 tbsp | Pure honey | 15 ml |
| 2 | Cloves, whole | 2 |
| 1 3-inch | Cinnamon stick | 1 3-inch |
| 2 pieces | Crystallized ginger, chopped | 2 pieces |
| dash | Sea salt | dash |

### Method:

Place all ingredients in a saucepan and bring to a boil. Reduce heat to a simmer and cook 20 minutes. Strain into a pitcher and serve warm.
**Yields 4 - 6 servings.**

### Apples and Apple Cider

Every day you brush your teeth to remove plaque buildup. Just like plaque on your teeth, LDL or "bad cholesterol" builds up in your arteries. Recently, researchers at the University of California-Davis have found that apples and apple cider helps to prevent the harmful build-up of arterial plaque.

# Sunny Summer Lemonade

## Variation

**Ginger-infused lemonade**

Add 2 tbsp of chopped ginger when adding sugar to water. When cooled, strain before final step of adding lemon juice.

*A delicious, tart and sweet lemonade made with your backyard patio in mind.*

### Ingredients:

| | | |
|---|---|---|
| 2 cups | Lemon juice | 500 ml |
| 1 cup | Granulated cane sugar or pure honey | 250 ml |
| 6 cups | Water | 1.5 L |

### Method:

Heat water in a saucepan and add sugar and cook until dissolved. Remove from heat and cool. Stir lemon juice into cooled sugar syrup. Place in a pitcher and chill until serving. Serve over ice with lemon slices to garnish. **Yields 6 - 8 servings.**

# Top 10 Reasons to *Buy Organic*

## 1. *Protect Future Generations*

*"We have not inherited the Earth from our fathers; we are borrowing it from our children."*

– Lester Brown

The average child receives four times more exposure than an adult to at least eight widely used cancer-causing pesticides in food. Food choices you make now will impact your child's future health.

## 2. *Prevent Soil Erosion*

The Soil Conservation Service estimates more than 3 billion tonnes of topsoil are eroded from the United States croplands each year. That means soil erodes seven times faster than it's built up naturally. Soil is the foundation of the food chain in organic farming. However, in conventional farming, the soil is used more as a medium for holding plants in a vertical position so they can be chemically fertilized. As a result, American farms are suffering from the worst soil erosion in history.

## 3. *Protect Water Quality*

Water makes up 2/3 of our body mass and covers 3/4 of the planet. The U.S. Environmental Protection Agency (EPA) estimates pesticides – some cancer causing – contaminate the groundwater in 38 states, polluting the primary source of drinking water for more than half the country's population.

## 4. *Save Energy*

American farms have changed drastically in the last three generations, from family-based small businesses dependant on human energy to large-scale factory farms. Modern farming uses more petroleum than any other single industry, consuming 12 % of the country's total energy supply. More energy is now used to produce synthetic fertilizers than to till, cultivate and harvest all the crops in the US. Organic farming is still based on labor-intensive practices such as hand weeding and green manure and crop covers instead of synthetic fertilizers to support soil.

## 5. *Keep Chemicals Off Your Plate*

Many pesticides approved for use by the EPA were registered long before extensive research linking these chemicals to cancer and other diseases had been established. Now the EPA considers 60% of all herbicides, 90% of all fungicides and 30% of all insecticides carcinogenic. The bottom line is that pesticides are poisons designed to kill living organisms and can also harm humans. In addition to cancer, pesticides are implicated in birth defects, nerve damage and genetic mutations.

## 6. *Protect Farm Workers*

A U.S. National Cancer Institute study found that farmers exposed to herbicides had six times more risk than non-farmers of contracting cancer. In California, reported pesticide poisonings among farm workers have risen an average of 14% a year since 1973 and doubled between 1975 and

1985. Field workers suffer the highest rates of occupational illness in the state. Farm worker health is also a serious problem in developing nations, where pesticide use can be poorly regulated. An estimated 1 million people are poisoned annually by pesticides.

## 7. Help Small Farmers

Although more and more large-scale farms are making the conversion to organic practices, most organic farms are small, independently owned family farms of fewer than 100 acres. It's estimated the United States has lost more than 650,000 family farms in the past decade. And with the U.S. Department of Agriculture predicting that half of this country's farm production will come from 1% of farms by 2000, organic farming could be one of the few survival tactics left for family farms.

## 8. Support a True Economy

Although organic foods might seem more expensive than conventional foods, conventional food prices don't reflect hidden costs borne by taxpayers, including nearly $74 billion in federal subsidies in 1998. Other hidden costs include pesticide regulation and testing, hazardous waste disposal and cleanup, and environmental damage. For instance, if you add in the environmental and social costs of irrigation to a head of lettuce, its price would range between $2 and $3.

## 9. Promote Biodiversity

Mono-cropping is the practice of planting large plots of land with the same crop year after year. While this approach tripled farm production between 1950 and 1970, the lack of natural diversity of plant life had left the soil lacking in natural minerals and nutrients. To replace the nutrients, chemical fertilizers are used, often in increasing amounts. Single crops are also much more susceptible to pests, making farmers more reliant on pesticides. Despite a tenfold increase in the use of pesticides between 1947 and 1974, crop losses due to insects have doubled – partly because some insects have become genetically resistant to certain pesticides.

## 10. Taste Better Flavour

There's a good reason why many chefs use organic foods in their recipes – they taste better. Organic farming starts with the nourishment of the soil, which eventually leads to the nourishment of the plant and ultimately, our palates.

*Excerpted from an article by Sylvia Tawse, Marketing Coordinator for Alfalfa's Markets in Boulder, Denver and Vail, CO.*

# Bean *Appétit*: Cooking with Beans

*Cooking with beans is easier than you may think. You can create imaginative, delicious and nutritious meals for your family with very little work.*

## Tips and Techniques

- Rinse well and drain beans before you cook them.
- Beans cook faster if soaked overnight (12 to 24 hours).
- 1 cup of dry beans yields 2 1/4 cups of cooked beans.

- Make sure beans are always covered with ample water when cooking.
- For a quick soak, bring beans to a boil, let sit 2 hours.
- To improve digestibility of beans – after first boil, drain and rinse off foam (produced by gases being released from the beans). Add new water.

- Turn a pot of beans into a stew by adding chopped vegetables for the last 1/2 hour.
- Experiment with herbs. Dill weed, bay leaves and celery seed are great with beans.
- Cooked beans will keep 4 to 5 days in the refrigerator.

## Cooking time for beans

| 1 Cup Beans | Water | Soaked Time | Unsoaked Time |
|---|---|---|---|
| Adzuki Beans | 2 1/2 cups | 60 mins | 120 - 180 mins |
| Black (Turtle) Beans | 3 cups | 60 mins | 120 - 180 mins |
| Chick peas or Garbanzo Beans | 4 cups | 120 mins | 180 - 240 mins |
| Fava Beans | 2 1/2 cups | 60 mins | 120 - 180 mins |
| Great Northern Beans | 3 1/2 cups | 120 mins | 120 - 180 mins |
| Dark Kidney Beans | 3 cups | 90 mins | 120 - 180 mins |
| Lentils – Green/French | 3 cups | no soaking | 40 mins |
| Lentils – Red/Yellow | 3 cups | 20 mins | 20 mins |
| Baby Lima Beans | 2 1/2 cups | 45 mins | 90 mins |
| Mung Beans | 3 1/2 cups | 60 mins | 90 mins |
| Navy Beans | 3 cups | 90 mins | 90 mins |
| Split Green Peas | 3 cups | no soaking | 60 mins |
| Split Yellow Peas | 3 cups | no soaking | 60 mins |
| Pinto Beans | 3 cups | 90 mins | 120 mins |
| Soy Beans | 3 cups | 60 mins | 60 mins |
| Beans Soup Mix | 5 cups | 120 mins | 180 mins |
| Lentil Soup Mix | 6 cups | no soaking | 40 mins |
| Organic Soup Mix | 6 cups | 60 mins | 120 mins |

# Great Grains: Cooking with Grains

*Try cooking with different grains. You can create imaginative, delicious and nutritious meals for your family with very little work.*

## Tips and Techniques

- Rinse and drain grains before you cook them.
- Cook grains by bringing to a boil and then reducing to the lowest heat possible. In most cases, cover the grains while they cook. Except for rices, it's recommended to stir grains while they are simmering.

- Instead of water, try using vegetable, chicken or fish stock.
- Add vegetables to your grains! In a heavy pot sauté onions, celery, peppers, even carrots! Then add water, bring to a boil and add grains.
- Organic grains are grown in well-balanced soils that harvest healthy plants with a higher nutritional value.

- If your grains and beans are not softening after a long cooking time, the problem could be their age!

Even beans and grains have an expiry date – buy in small quantities and replace often, (anything older than a year, should be replaced).

## Cooking time for grains

| 1 Cup Grains | Water | Time | 1 Cup Grains | Water | Time |
|---|---|---|---|---|---|
| Amaranth* | 2 cups | 20 mins | Rice – Brown Basmati* | 2 cups | 25 mins |
| Barley – Hulled | 3 cups | 90 mins | Rice – Sweet Brown* | 2 cups | 50 mins |
| Barley – Pearled | 2 1/2 cups | 60 mins | Rice – Arborio* | 1 1/4 cups | 30 mins |
| Barley – Pot | 3 cups | 50 - 60 mins | Rice – White Jasmine* | 2 cups | 20 mins |
| Buckwheat – Kasha* | 2 cups | 20 mins | Rice – Sushi* | 1 1/2 cups | 20 mins |
| Buckwheat – Hulled & Whole* | 2 cups | 20 mins | Rice – Wild* | 2 cups | 50 mins |
| Corn Grits (also called Polenta) | 3 cups | 20 mins | Rice – Wild, Blend* | 2 cups | 50 mins |
| Kamut® Kernels | 3 cups | 90 mins | Rye Kernels | 2 cups | 30 mins |
| Kamut® Flakes | 2 cups | 15 - 20 mins | Rye Flakes | 3 cups | 30 mins |
| Millet* | 2 1/2 cups | 30 mins | Soy Flakes | 4 cups | 10 mins |
| Oats – Hulled | 2 cups | 40 mins | Spelt Flakes | 3 cups | 20 - 25 mins |
| Oats – Quick | 2 cups | 5 mins | Spelt Kernels | 3 cups | 120 mins |
| Oats – Rolled (Slow Cooking) | 2 cups | 30 mins | Triticale | 2 1/2 cups | 60 mins |
| Oats – Steel Cut | 3 cups | 40 mins | Triticale Flakes | 2 cups | 20 mins |
| Quinoa* | 2 cups | 20 mins | Wheat – Couscous | 2 1/2 cups | 10 mins |
| Rice – Brown (short & long grain)* | 2 cups | 25 mins | Wheat – Hard Red (berries) | 3 cups | 120 mins |
| Rice – White Basmati* | 2 cups | 15 mins | Wheat – Soft White | 3 cups | 120 mins |

*(\*All grains with this symbol are gluten-free.)*

# Index

# Index

# Diane Shaskin's Bio

For Diane, it's always been about the food, whether cooking for her family and friends, finding a tiny, perfect restaurant, or exploring the markets of Provençe. Her passion for good food began as a child in Southern Alberta, with a steady diet of homemade Ukrainian foods such as borscht with sour cream and bread. Her love of new flavours and classic favourites has helped her make friends wherever she has travelled. She is the co-founder and Marketing Director for Planet Organic Markets and is married to the President, Mark Craft. They have a wonderful 6-year-old son.